AF349968

MANON

MANON

FEATHERS
2 Months and 12 Days. Notes

Edition Patrick Frey

N° 310

For my husband Sikander from Bhicknapahari, who has been my unwavering companion for so many years.

Dear Reader,

Last spring I rediscovered these long forgotten notes. The distance of a few years gives me the courage to entrust you with Feathers.

There is mention in these notes of a film to be made for movie theatres. And talk of a biography that a journalist was planning to write.
    Like so many other things, I cancelled both projects.
    I think they frightened me.

The film was finally made after all, years later, but for television, directed by a woman, which is what I actually always wanted.

The biography, well, I'm getting older, we'll see…

There's also talk of a book, *Einst war sie MISS RIMINI* (She Was Once Miss Rimini), published shortly after making these notes. And of an art project, still extremely vague, that finally came about early in 2018, titled Der *Wachsaal* (The Observation Room). [A play on the double meaning of the German word wach: "to watch over" and "awake."]

Feathers consists of diary entries I made at the request of the filmmaker, in order to give him a little insight into both my current and past lives.

Several of the people mentioned have since died.
   This diary ends on the day I decided against doing the film.

Manon, Spring 2019

2005

22 February

Women who do a balancing act on that extremely thin line between still being beautiful but no longer young have always been particularly appealing to me, perhaps because their fall is so close, so inevitable.

It reminds me of Bette Davis in *All About Eve*, but also of the actress Charlotte Rampling, or of Jeanne Moreau. I could have knelt down in front of women like that because the fragility of their beauty had reached a breaking point.

Will I also look back at myself as compassionately someday?

The filmmaker wants me to keep a diary of sorts to give him an insight into my life, into the way I think, what I have on my mind, my concerns, or even my memories.

This is what brought me to start writing notes about the course of time. And about the course of my time.

23 February

If I were to reach the same age as my parents —they were not granted their statistically anticipated number of years—I would still have 12 years to live.

That's damned little for someone who has been so slow to learn how much fun it is to be alive.

"Officially" I'm a few years younger than my passport says, and have been so ever since the beginning of my artistic career when a newspaper didn't bother to confirm whether the birthdate they printed was correct. Other newspapers and reference works on art, like Wikipedia and Sikart, simply copied the wrong date. So I have quite innocently gained time.

I was still young in those days. There was no need to conceal my age. But even then I was already thinking about the future and thought I might someday be pleased about gaining a few years, so I let it be.

Or have I actually ended up losing time? Because I will have lived six years less than people think?

> *"Ne me demandez pas mon âge,*
> *il change tout le temps."*

Don't ask me how old I am because it keeps changing. That's what the author and humorist Alphons Allais once said.

By contrast, French writer and feminist Benoîte Groult, now 85 years old and still going strong, remarked: "Only as of eighty does a French-woman stand by her age. She is in a gray zone between forty and eighty."
You can look at it that way, too.

There is going to be a panel discussion tomorrow organized by the Mayor's Office of Zurich, titled "Age—a Drag or a Delight?" A panel of reputable men and women, like an ex-city councilor, an ex-newspaper editor of the NZZ, an ex-director of retirement homes, the municipal physician of Zurich, still in office, and an ex-social work director turned writer, who is the sister of one of our federal councilors—and then me, invited to join all of these dignitaries!
Maybe as a kind of exotic extra, a spot of color? Because I'm still far from being an ex-anything.

First and foremost, presumably, as the creator of the 50-part photo series *Einst war sie MISS RIMINI* (She Was Once MISS RIMINI).

You could also say as a fictional ex-MISS RIMINI, because I myself—as Manon—don't appear in that project.

24 February
My parents died some time ago, so I've moved up to the first row.

Ah, death is breathing down our necks; to be more precise, he's our constant companion.

I'm acutely aware of that, it makes time precious. And, occasionally, beautiful.

It often really scares me.

It would be wonderful if age went hand-in-hand with mental growth.

Because the prospect of mental deterioration is much more frightening to me than physical decay. Not being able to express yourself and losing the respect of those around you: that's what happened to my father who was a scholar and lost his entire "capital," which also meant he was no longer capable of benefiting from his experience.

However, in the process I learned:

The soul remains intact and therefore vulnerable, until the very end!

I've acquired several things over the years: a great faculty for happiness that I never used to have, happiness that is entirely independent of other people. Or the peace of mind to rise above everyday adversities because time is too precious to waste on minor hassles.

Years ago—it was 1993—I designed a large installation about death. It was called *Die Philosophie im Boudoir* (Philosophy in the Boudoir), after de Sade's offbeat title, *La Philosophie dans le boudoir*. I hadn't read the book, but the title was inspiring.

Especially since it was a nod to another exhibition: my very first appearance on the art scene, namely, the presentation of my bedroom, that was in 1974, I called it *Das lachsfarbene Boudoir* (The Salmon-Colored Boudoir). I was saying goodbye to a great love at the time, to a marriage in fact, and it was the beginning of an entirely new phase of my life.

But the above-mentioned work of 1993, consisting of eight massive, chrome dissecting tables, was about definitive departure—people important to me who had already taken their leave.

These dissecting tables—they were solid, glossy, and gorgeous to look at—had been lent to me from the Institute of Forensic Medicine under one condition: if a catastrophe were to occur, I would have to return them instantly.

But everything went well.

Having the opportunity to tackle challenging issues and transform them into an artistic act means a lot to me.

Still in bed with the tail end of a minor flu, I'll get up towards evening and see how I can manage the panel discussion despite a slight fever.

Last year I decided that I would take my little digital camera with me every day and shoot at least one photograph. In contrast to my previous work, I didn't want to stage anything, I simply wanted to capture what life has to offer. Everyday things, my animals, still lifes, the lake, the unusual and the usual. According to my husband's calculations, the result was several thousand pictures in the course of a year. Occasionally I would get really worked up when I came across a subject that seemed particularly attractive as seen through my personal filter.

I didn't skip a single day; I even pressed the shutter release one evening after taking an anesthetic.

Tellingly, there are hardly any people in these pictures.

I'm extremely wary in that respect.

I want to try out something similar this year but in a different medium: I want to sit down at the computer every day and comment on my perfectly ordinary daily life, just what the filmmaker wants. If I had had a say when aptitudes were distributed, I would probably have selected writing. I have always envied writers. They are not burdened by bulky props; they can easily pursue their passion no matter where they are. Every time I move into a studio abroad, there are dozens of banana boxes to be unpacked. Documents, photographic equipment, backdrops, paint, notebooks, files of negatives, costumes, props, lighting, tripods, and on and on.

Early this morning I took a picture of a crow's nest. I discovered it yesterday in the fork of a barren tree, the tallest one at the entrance to "my" park. They are such fascinating creatures, industriously flying about and breaking twigs off other trees to prepare for raising their brood in March. Astonishingly, their nest is exposed to rain and snow and I wonder if they will survive the storms in spring.
    I don't know if I've just been blind or whether there used to be fewer carrion crows (that's what they call our indigenous species). In any

case, I took only rudimentary notice of them. Once I saw two of them pecking away at an injured sparrow that wasn't dead yet. I didn't like them anymore for a while after that.

25 February
Survived last night pretty well, with the help of some medication. Before that, scrambled to fix the torn seam of my flea market coat with safety pins, tied a turban out of egg-shell colored fabric, and put on gala makeup. I wanted to look glamorous, especially for the evening's topic.

We had barely reached the entrance when my husband and I were turned away because we had our dog along, our "Parisian." The doorman finally relented because I had to go on stage.
   It certainly wouldn't hurt to animate such totally ritualized events with something that's alive, something unexpected!

The ex-director of education—apparently already 80 years old—was not there; he wasn't well. I used to consider him one of my personal "enemies," specifically, an enemy of progressive and rebellious young people during the revolts in Zurich. Wouldn't have minded finding out if his rigidity had mellowed over the years. The ex-NZZ editor simply didn't show up. The first thing the moderator—I had seen her on television—asked us was how old we would like to be if we could choose.

Unsurprisingly, nobody wanted to be twenty or thirty anymore but rather at least around forty. There was a lot of laughter. We thoroughly enjoyed ourselves and the audience—a lot of people turned up—did, too.

The municipal physician talked about medical matters, which, as we all know, have changed: people enjoy relatively good health as they get older and no longer spend so much time being infirm and dependent.

One question addressed to me was: Ms. Manon, how do you feel today with your beauty slowly declining? A woman from the audience called out: She's even more beautiful now.

I've often found that women give me especially loving looks.

To my great surprise I discovered the musician and composer Stefan W. sitting in one of the front rows. He had just been young a minute ago. We were both young when a brief affair united us. The affection is still there.

Later I saw my sister, who was born shortly after me. Beautiful and radiant, she told me that she occasionally feels like retiring early. If I didn't know better, I would assume she was in her mid-forties. Since our father died, we have only seen one another at public events although we live in the same city. I need distance.

I bonded instantly with the over 70-year-old writer, who is always mentioned with a hyphenated last name—probably on the recommendation of her publisher. Just recently, I had come across her latest book. She was once an active radical leftist, the exact opposite of her brother, who currently holds the highest political office in Switzerland. I was touched when she told me about her brain operation 10 years ago, after which she "lost half of her face." Although barely perceptible, it is still slightly paralyzed.

A warm, intelligent woman. We will certainly meet again.

I also feel a greater affinity with the left than with the right.

Her inflammatory partner in the early days, Elena F., once a left-wing city councilor from Milan, mother of my soulmate, I call him the Salamander, is dying. He wrote to me that this seems to make time stand still for him. Every

day he takes the same two-hour drive: Bern–
Zurich–Triemli Hospital, and back again. The
tough, 92-year-old body is still resisting death.
It had long been spared.

Memories of my father between life and death
—it took a week. I slept on the floor next to his
bed, didn't want to leave him alone. I wanted
to meet his death personally—my time stood
still, too. Occasionally I left the darkened room
with the dog—an island, unreal, separated, a
very small self-contained universe, there was
no outside anymore, only the wheezing breath
of someone dying—and then, in sudden day-
light, I would be overcome by an abrupt, fierce
feeling of happiness: the sun, the wind on my
face, life in full bloom.

My father resisted, his whole body was full of
tension and fear, his last breath a very long,
immeasurably sad sigh. It was not a "beautiful
death."
    I think my father would have liked to live
longer but not in the way he had to spend the
final years of his life.

My opinion on this evening, one I have already
advanced on another occasion, was more or
less as follows:

I have an extremely precise image of myself, of what I might look like as a very old woman, an image I can certainly say yes to. On the other hand, I have absolutely no idea who I will be between now and then, I simply cannot envision it. For the longest time I couldn't understand why until I realized there are no images, no models anymore.

I've spent years exploring the subject of identity. When I turned forty, I considered the subject closed. I decided that there's something wrong with anybody who does not know by then who he is, what he wants, how he is perceived, and to what extent his inner and outer being coincide.

And now, lo and behold, a few years later, there they are, these questions, cropping up unasked, and probably for all of us. There are compelling reasons for that. The generation before us, especially the women, lived and aged differently and died earlier, so we have no role models, no examples. We are rediscovering ourselves all over again while still participating actively in life; looking after grandchildren is not our highest priority.

The subject of death was entirely disregarded.

"Death does not concern us, because as long as we exist, death is not here. And when it does come, we no longer exist."

I will try to abide by this wonderfully wise statement.

I discover that the profoundly life-affirming Greek philosopher Epicurus already wrote it 300 years before Christ.

My husband's back from the doctor. Surprisingly, nothing seems to be wrong with his inner organs despite opiates required for years to relieve daily pain caused by whiplash. The pain and the medication were never an issue for us, they were simply part of everyday life. But he has since largely weaned himself from the drugs and has learned to cope with the impairment.

When we first met, I was the one who couldn't function a single day—and hadn't been able to for years—without complex medical cocktails. He was okay with it; that was just the way it was. Then my withdrawal followed, which ultimately took seven, long, hard years.

26 February
Saturday is my day. No appointments, ever. I steer clear of events on Saturday. The weekend

shopping and other unavoidables are followed by a walk to the newsstand in the late afternoon and then to my favorite longstanding hangout: the library.

More often than not, I take a list of books along, but I also just wander around, pulling out a book here, leafing through another one there. Then home to my mirrored room with a huge stack of biographies, art books, novels and non-fiction. Fan them all out on my big bed, along with a platter of canapés, and lamps around the bed that make for beautiful lighting. Then crawl under the old fluffy blanket, the cats and the dog lie down too, they are used to the ritual. Next step, sniffing at each of the books, leafing through them and reading a bit until one grabs me.

The wintry leafless beech in front of my window—it planted itself years ago in the earth of an unused clay pot and is now showered with TLC, which includes embellishing it like a Christmas tree with round balls of birdseed. It's been requisitioned by an ever-growing family of chirping and twittering sparrows and brims with life every half hour.

Later in the park they'll become so tame that they eat out of my hand. I love those cheerful survivors.

In summer my cats occasionally drag one into our flat. Several times I've had the privilege of doing one in after the bird has been irreparably injured and the cats won't finish it off.

Trees live longer than people do. One day my beech is going to find a home in the garden of some nice people. It's already arranged.

Suddenly a memory of pigeons surfaces, a couple of them nesting behind in the shutters of the flat where I used to live in the old town of Zurich, a converted attic. I can still hear them cooing; right at the head of my bed. It sounded incredibly erotic and was accessory to many a moment of lovemaking. One day my Siamese cat laid a cock pigeon at my feet. His wife cooed and called and lamented for three whole days; it was heartbreaking.

The widows usually don't mate again.

Reading! Thanks to the flu, I have enjoyed the luxury of lying in bed reading for a whole week, and it's glorious. No guilty conscience, no work pressure. Sometimes I dream of spending a whole winter all alone in the country with noth-ing but a stack of books in a simple house with wooden walls and I wouldn't mind having a wood-burning tiled stove either. Maybe I'll treat myself to that someday.

Bookstores have always exerted a magical attraction and, incidentally, stationers, too, and perfume shops because of the packaging and the fragrances and lingerie shops, the really luxurious ones, especially in Paris or Milan.

And flea markets, too, all over the world. I love them. I love discovering rare books or curios.

The older I get the more I enjoy a sense of serenity that used to be alien to me. It's as if a lifework has come about. In addition to the exhibited, published, and more or less known photographs, probably a hundred or so, there are file folders full of negatives and subject matters that have never been sorted or used in some way.

One day I'll have to do something about them.

27 February

Arm in arm we are off to the Terrasse, a restaurant where my husband and I go for breakfast on Sundays, always sitting at table number 18 in the bay window of this beautifully designed room with its light blue ceiling and painted clouds to be pampered by thoughtful waiters. I take a photograph of a gilded head sculpted by Otto Müller, which has been assigned a conspicuous place on a gray plinth in front of a lilac colored wall. A few years before Müller died, he told me that he had molded a large ear after a photograph of me because my ears were so precisely formed. His source image was probably the portrait of me bald, on the roof of a building in Paris with the city's high-rises in the background.

Not much later, I met his partner in an entirely different connection—Trudi Demut, a sculptress, always reserved and modest. We often sat together at Charlotte Schmid's, a graphic designer and the best hostess in Zurich. I will never forget the unparalleled Christmas decoration she designed for the Bahnhofstrasse in Zurich, millions of warm yellow light bulbs.

Last year, from 1 January 2004 to 1 January 2005, I called Sundays my "harvesting day." The week's photographs were imported from the digital camera to the computer—my husband did that—then sorted and finally a selection printed out, cropped, dated, numbered, and filed in file folders. I think there was only one day on which I came up with only one photograph, but countless days with hundreds and more pictures. In any case, every Sunday was filled with this task until well into the evening and often Monday, and sometimes even Tuesday, had to follow suit. I called them "fast pictures throughout the year."

I want to apply the same discipline to sitting down at the computer every day and typing in at least one note. What is being done at the moment, what I remember spontaneously, what seems worth mentioning, just as uncensored as last year's photographs, and entirely apart from whether the filmmaker will read it or whether some other use will be found for it. I have always enjoyed writing but I know perfectly well that my talent lies elsewhere.

A little at loose ends, I sit here today in front of eight files stuffed full of the days' photographs. I told the filmmaker Edith Jud about it. She once made a TV program about my work: Forever Young. She called this work "a second trail," in contrast to my staged pictures. I liked that.

The most moving subjects for me are those of my dead animals, my greyhound Arletty, slender, drenched in blood, run over by a car right in front of us, we had to have her put down. Little Daisy and later Missy who went through thick and thin with me for years, died of old age. Lying on my bed, decorated with flowers, the cats sitting next to her in silence for a whole evening. Or my tomcat Gigolo, put in a plastic container at the crematory, cold and already beginning to putrefy.

But also a rat, its throat bitten—"my" crows had dropped it in flight—and other animals, too, including a headless pigeon surrounded by a sea of feathers, a couple of sparrows, and a blackbird caught in a storm and drowned in a basin. A rabbit, maybe three days old, naked with pink skin, still alive when I found it in a meadow as well as a white dwarf rabbit, already stiff, found by chance in a wastebasket and later buried in the park.

It's as if dead animals were attracted to me.

For years I felt that my animal photographs don't belong in the art context.

But you can't separate them from the every-day pictures.

28 February
Early this morning the first tracks in the fresh snow: the tiny footprints of a small dog, you would almost think it was a big bird, our "Parisian" has slightly bigger ones.

Received the cover blurb for my publication due to come out in spring. The writer, a lovely tall young woman with long blonde hair and a soft voice, has summed up my work beautiful-ly in just a few poetic sentences.

She will also have to submit an outline of the themes for my biography to the same publish-er by the middle of March. It's scheduled for one or two years later.

In a subsequent telephone conversation, she raises a question that I am always being asked: what happens to all the drawings and notes that accumulate in preparing for a photo series or an installation? Or to the countless experiments with backgrounds and lighting for the camera? Do I want to exhibit that some-day? Can one look at the material?

Well, as soon as a project is completed, everything that preceded it gets thrown away with a tremendous sense of relief. To me, show-ing the sketches is like leaving the house with only half my makeup on.

That's also a big problem regarding the film that's going to be made: I don't like anybody looking over my shoulder when I work. I can't take it.

The journalist tells me afterwards that her childhood was overshadowed by having a seriously ill father so that she never had a chance to "live it up" like everybody else. She stayed at home until he died, by which time she was 27. Now I understand why she is so happy to be studying a second time in London, although married in Zurich. She has to make up for the carefree student life that she missed the first time around.

An invitation to an opening and dinner from an artist dear to me, who lives in the French part of Switzerland but is basically a nomad. I have intimate memories of a time over twenty years ago when he was practically unknown and I had just come back from Paris and was in the process of becoming better known (he has since far surpassed me and become world-famous).

His hair is still long, thick, and black though he no longer wears it loose the way I liked it so much. Once a muscular rower, he has barely gained weight, and his unusually beautiful body is now fifty years old. There are wonderful photos of him that I took in some cheap hotel, where was that? And pretty pictures of both of us undressed but very chaste, taken with the self-timer. Maybe they will be seen someday but not before we're eighty or dead.

Why didn't I stay with him? There was never an unkind word. He was so carefree and I took everything so seriously.

And then I met my current husband.

Recently I took some pictures of the artist again. He was re-enacting one of his early performances at an art venue. Only insiders had seen it at the time. I had never seen it. It was so mischievous and charming.

1 March
Phoned the Salamander, lifelong friend and partner for seven wild years. His mother Elena F. is still alive. She's paralyzed and not conscious all the time.

They've put her on an IV, even though she has a living will and doesn't want any life-prolonging procedures.

It seems that a living will is not fully binding, for instance, you have to specify at exactly which point tube feeding should be stopped. Who thinks of details like that when you're writing a living will?

Lots of snow, lots of sun.
An unusually cold, beautiful winter day.

Bought a small sofa at the local thrift shop. Doesn't look like much yet but with a few modifications, it'll look fabulous in our "Frascati Haus" apartment.

That's always been my greatest talent: making something out of nothing.

Which applies to everything: rooms, furniture, clothing, jewelry, and ultimately me.

There was only room enough in the car for the soft parts of the sofa. The metal frame was too big. I shouldered it and carried it home, icy streets and all.

I'm going to make a few changes. It will look elegant.

Actually, I have an exhibition I could propose. What's holding me up is that I'm at a complete loss because I can't figure out how to present the pictures. The photographs would work much better in a very lively, very comprehensive book.

Actually, I have several ideas for exhibitions. For instance, "Never Shown Pictures" has been a potential theme for a long time.

What I would like to tackle after the representation of over fifty different women in the MISS RIMINI series, yes, that could be fascinating: making a convincing man out of myself and taking pictures of him.

If I succeed, it would turn the identity issue upside down.

In the early days of the women's movement, "masculinity" and "femininity" were supposedly a consequence of socialization. Later, this radical thought was toned down a bit.

In Paris, with all my hair shaved off and living in an Arab neighborhood, the men thought I was a transvestite, a man dressed like a woman. I liked that.

The press called me "androgynous." I would have loved to be both masculine and feminine, extremely feminine, actually, because I wanted to try out every conceivable experience.

I had long suspected that the figure of "Manon," gutsy seductress and man-eater with all her highly sophisticated props, was actually disguising someone entirely different. Namely, an ordinary girl, intensely serious, but above all scarred by her mother, wounded for life, an emotional invalid.

The way I was would never be enough, never. So how do you have to be in order to exist?

It was quite simply a matter of survival when I later created the so-called fictitious character of "Manon."

I realize that in hindsight.

It has long since become totally irrelevant that my parents never wanted to accept this character. But at least the public noticed her.

That's why the question of identity has always preyed on my mind, and probably will for the rest of my life.

In her postscript to *Einst war sie MISS RIMINI,* the journalist writes that even though I take pictures of myself, they are never self-portraits.

I think she's mistaken. Although the figure of Manon was intentionally omitted in this new work with so many different figures of women, I never had the feeling of being in costume. I am the clochard, certainly the mental patient, the society dame, or the woman stranded in her resignation: just one title change could have altered the course of my life.

I don't think I would have been the kind of actress that watches from outside how this or that person moves; I would probably have tried to find corresponding facets in myself. I think I could only have played myself.

Maybe I should describe how the series of photographs came about:

On the basis of drawings and notes, I would do up one woman a day, a different person every day with her envisioned fate as a former beauty queen on the Italian Riviera. Her hair, clothing, and face had to be fixed up first, followed by deciding on gestures, facial expression, and pose.

I often represented women who seemed older than I am and occasionally also younger. But there was no room for vanity.

My husband was working days at a job that had nothing to do with art. Then down to the basement in the evening, Frascati Haus, to set up the tripod and camera, a movable mirror for control, my drawing on the floor between my partner and me as the character. Usually worked through the night and if we were lucky, we knew towards morning that the picture "worked." If not, we returned to the same subject the following night. Sleep was not much of a priority during those weeks, or rather months; we got more and more irritable and often had fights. After the fiftieth character we were shot, both physically and mentally. For the first time, I wondered whether our relationship could survive such a marathon.

On the other hand, I can only work with someone I feel really close to because I absolutely hate being photographed except when I'm in charge. Every professional photographer who has ever wanted to take a picture for a newspaper knows what I'm talking about: I'm embarrassed and very difficult.

So I often wondered how I would ever manage without my husband. Besides, technically and digitally he's also better than I am, and much more patient, and on top of that, he's convinced that the work has to be done.

Friends thought it must be fascinating for a man to meet up with a different woman when he comes home every evening. Actually, my partner was always much too tired to appreciate it.

2 March
Bright winter sun in the morning at the charming new lakeside café. Dog lovers' den. Don't know the names of the regulars but, for the most part, we do know those of their dogs.

Two puffed up blackbirds are looking for something to eat under the blanket of snow.

Call from Bern. They want to screen my 1977 video, *Der Tod ist unser aller Gigolo*, again, and publish a catalog with it. The title is borrowed from Baudrillard. Which made the art museum ask a lot of questions.

The gigolo as a "constant companion" of elderly women, and not infrequently elderly men as well… In other words: death is everybody's gigolo. I thought the Parisian philosopher and word artist had expressed it extraordinarily well. I was obviously already thinking about death in those days too.

Which reminds me of an Italian journalist I met in Genoa who has written quite a bit about my work and quoted the exact same philosopher in the introduction to a catalog, titled, *Soggetto e oggetto, desiderio e seduzione nell' opera di Manon*.

> "Le sujet ne peut que désirer,
> seul l'objet peut séduire."
>
> Jean Baudrillard

My first video is practically static. That's not accidental; movement is not my medium. Maybe that's part of why I balk at the planned and actually half-begun movie. Oh, that movie: do I even want it? Do I need it? The very thought of it makes me bristle.
    I'm suppressing it brilliantly at the moment.

On the other hand, I remember that I later used the term "gigolo" again in another title; it was an installation. It was set up as a window display in a gallery in Lucerne, specifically for the night, you could only see it from the dark street. The gallery was in an out-of-the-way, nonresidential, and slightly spooky industrial neighborhood.

Seen in the big window: a stuffed wolf (from the Museum of Natural History in St. Gallen) attached to a heavy iron chain suspended from the ceiling. A big mirror ball at the other end of the same chain. A bundle of love letters from my personal inventory. The little scene was pretty dramatically illuminated by a single spotlight. The following was written in chalk on a big blackboard in the background:

for Chet Baker
and Jim Morrison
and Hervé Guibert and
Truman Capote
and Jacques Brel and
Urs Lüthi and Philippe
Petit and Pierre
Clémenti and Jim
Jarmusch and Tom
Waits and Philip
Roth and Jean Cocteau

After pushing a buzzer from outside, people were startled by the overwhelming voice of the singer Yma Sumac resounding in the quiet, empty darkness of that wasteland.

It was an ice-cold evening in late autumn with pouring rain. Before leaving home, I already knew it: this evening was going to be an all-time low in my artistic career. There would probably be hardly anybody there. That's a rather sobering experience: knowing ahead of time, today, tonight I'm probably going to be practically alone with my work. "Now or never," I figured, and decked myself out with exceptional care—I had never made such a conspicuous appearance at an opening.

And sure enough: There was nobody there except for a few faithful friends and a few Manon fans huddled under big umbrellas... And I knew: it wasn't the weather, it wasn't the location—it was me.
　　I simply wasn't "trending" at the time.
　　I couldn't have cared less.

Practically none of my shows is etched in my memory like that one. It could have been yesterday: I hear the echoing steps and the pounding rain and then suddenly, this stunning voice.

The atmosphere was intense, electrifying, more so than at many successful openings.

For a long time I've been mulling over the series of photographs I mentioned above. Several times I've tackled it and then dropped it again. Happens to me every time. It hasn't really matured, but it's "germinating." There are already sketches, descriptions, and source images.

I'm wondering whether I should ask the makeup artist, the one who made me look bald for the cancer patients in the "Rimini" series—it was the only transformation I couldn't do myself, and it looked authentic—anyway, I'm wondering if I should have this expert make a man out of me.

(Regarding the bald pate: this time, on my way back to the studio—I'm no longer the young girl I was in Paris when I really shaved off all my hair—the reaction was completely different: brief, embarrassed glances. Did people think it was chemotherapy?)

So one could set up a video camera and film the gradual change and take step-by-step photos at the same time. As a "man" I would create a new sequence of photographs very different from last time, with these typical male poses that I know so well: sitting, standing, walking, gesticulating… This work would essentially take the question of identity ad absurdum. That might appeal to me.

First I want to see if I can create the metamorphosis myself. I would love to try it.

I envision the work in black-and-white.

Would the first thing be to sacrifice my pageboy haircut for the sake of something more manly? Something like the haircut I had for the last two photo series that I made towards the end of my three-year stay in Paris? One of them was called *Elektrokardiogram 304 / 303* and the other one *Die graue Wand oder 36 schlaflose Nächte* (The Grey Wall or 36 Sleepless Nights). (One of the pictures graces the cover of my second book published in Bern, and I certainly won't hide the fact that it was awarded a prize as one of the "Most Beautiful Swiss Books.")

The new project would probably be a rather prolonged affair.

I would have to bandage my breasts. I would need an undershirt with sewed-in, organic looking shoulder pads, and men's clothing, largely from my partner who is not much taller than I am: I prefer eye level.

First I had the idea of designing two parallel series with the working title "Gender Studies," one as a woman with a typically female habitus and the other as a man with a typically male habitus.

Apropos gender studies: I'd give anything to study (continue studying) that discipline. The University in Zurich doesn't teach gender studies, only Freiburg and Geneva are progressive enough. That's my field. My subject.

Last winter, an art academy organized an event for which I designed an evening of pictures using the above motto. I've already been asked to do it again with a new set of students.

3 March
Outside early this morning in the midst of radiant sunshine a sentence occurred to me from one of my favorite films: Jim Jarmusch's *Down by Law*, 1986, a classic by now. Speaking to fellow convicts in a prison cell, the Italian Roberto Benigni says:

"It's a sad and a beautiful world."

In one of my former apartments, I painted it in white on a black wall behind my bed that was completely covered in red. There was a picture in some magazine of me and my husband prettily draped on the bed in front of it. I don't remember what the context was.

Someday I'm going to integrate this wonderfully true and poetic sentence into a work. I don't know where and how yet, but it will get done.

In the meantime, I'll have it engraved on a silver bangle.

Happiness and grief, always so close together.
Melancholy.

Mail from a longtime friend, totally depressed. He writes that he has "...no appointments, no friends, no plans." He says, "everything is over."

For a long time, actually all my life, I always felt that I had no home. Didn't belong anywhere. Outside of everything. Only now, after so many years, I seem to have found a place in what is called the art scene. And maybe someday in art history.

Just found out that Elena F. died. Her battle with death lasted a week.

Right after my father died, I lay down in bed with him, in his arms, where I had never lain before. Everything that had tortured me for years came gushing out in a torrent of tears: the futile longing to be noticed, to be accepted. The disappointment time and again over his lack of interest in me as a daughter, later as a person, still later as an artist. As soon as problems cropped up, I was sent away. First to a home for children, then to a boarding school (unforgettable his handshake at the railroad station, he had never touched me before), and then, at the age of 17, to a psychiatric clinic for many months. After that I never went home again.

Problems were outsourced.

He never found out how much my mother rejected me—instead of him, because she couldn't afford to rebuff him. She thought I was ugly.

In his final years, when he was losing his mind, I gradually became reconciled with him —although he couldn't realize it—and was there for him.

I learned to interpret my parents' behavior in terms of their own story. After they died and for the first time in my life, I put up a photograph of them in our apartment.

Now I no longer have any bad feelings. That gives me a sense of peace that I didn't have for many years.

To be fair, I must admit that I never read any of my father's books. They are scholarly works about economic and political relations and their content is alien to me. The most famous one is probably *Der arme Süden und der reiche Norden* (The Poor South and the Rich North); it became a reference work. After he died I stacked the books up in our apartment under a glass cube, it was a small installation, a tribute.

As a child, when people asked me what he did, I said, "He's a conomist." That's what it sounded like to me.

On television the other day a film about a very old Charlie Chaplin. On his 85th birthday in the interview, tired, scarred, captivating: "Death is coming slowly. And life is so beautiful."

A friend, she's a professor and teacher at an art academy, has to leave for a couple days, so she's bringing us her black cat tonight, a gentle old creature with amber eyes. I offered to help out as we only have three cats left in our household since Gigolo and Lulu died.

She told me that she has never lived with a man in her entire life, even though she was once married. And now at the age of sixty—she looks fifty—she still has no partner and she's looking for one. Trouble is: the minute a man realizes she's an intellectual, she is no longer perceived as a woman!

But she wants a relationship at all cost. Besides, she wants to retire early so that she can finally prove herself as an artist.

That makes me realize how lucky I am. For one thing, I've never been without someone who liked me and secondly, I've always been able to pursue my life as an artist. Money was often short but somehow I always managed to carry out my projects.

For a while I transformed men into women for good money and then took Polaroid pictures of them. I was so good at creating these "women" that I pocketed extra tips; as a "transformer" I'm the best.

In Paris once, I did a show as a transvestite on a small stage in a gay bar.

Occasionally I also went out with rich men who got a kick out of being seen with an unusual woman (with all my hair shaved off).

Including a very famous art collector who was living in Paris at the time and now lives in Germany and has just bequeathed his entire collection to a museum in a German city. He didn't see me as an artist, but most certaily as a woman, an exotic exemplar of humankind.

But I was used to that.

I met the art teacher at a shared exhibition and I like her. She's intelligent, pretty, lonely, and more than that, she hasn't got a single intimate friend.

That's tough.

She asked me if I'd ever taken LSD, if I ever had any sexual experience with women, well, I've always been curious, whether I think of myself as a feminist, goes without saying, always have.

4 March

The cat is here. Looks like it's not that simple, she kept us up all night. Luckily, I have a way with cats.

Oh, cats. My youngest sister died alone, with clenched fists, lips pressed closed, face distorted in pain. The small room, gloomy, close to the street but her tomcat, this big, timid, freedom-loving creature, red-streaked fur, who always jumped out of the ground floor window when visitors came, lying stretched out on her body, refusing to move, for hours, a whole day and a whole night. He had to be removed by force in order to take the body away.

They told me they put him to sleep.

I'm meeting the filmmaker in an hour for another meeting, having sent him the following email:

"The more I think about us and the film, the more I get the feeling that we haven't really established a close relationship. That's why neither you nor I will succeed in developing imaginative visions for this film. Maybe I've never really 'touched' you? Wouldn't this being touched by a person and their work be a prerequisite for collaboration? It seems to me that our few, short encounters got stuck on the surface, never really went into depth.

"And I still can't help feeling that maybe your mind is elsewhere. For example, I was totally astonished that you never looked at my monograph in some library and, in fact, that you didn't even know about it. You have never asked me about the work I've done so far and, to this day, I still don't know if you are familiar with it or not—probably not. You never wanted to look at photographs, for example, from the days when I was still a young model or when the local press turned me into their latest scandal. 'If Manon had been born in another century, they would have burned her at the stake.' A magazine actually published that subtitle in a several-page report about me. Wouldn't that be something worth talking about? Or… Is it possible that you haven't had the time to do any research so far?

"Incidentally, that's exactly what bothers me about your Derrida film (along with the indifference of the camerawork). The crew didn't get close to the subject. They probably thought that they could just trail after Jacques Derrida in his everyday life, step-by-step, and people would finally begin to understand him and particularly his work, but that didn't happen, precisely because they never established any mutual rapport. But I think there must be (and could have been) such a rapport. Otherwise, a film is pretty superfluous. Wouldn't you agree?

"Those are my thoughts about the film at the moment. If we do decide to collaborate for the next few months, we're really going to have to pull ourselves together.

"Maybe, in fact probably, we have a completely different vision of a potential film. I would like to have magical images, seduction, mystery, colors, stories, specially staged scenes, maybe based on earlier works of mine, I'm thinking for example of *The Artist Is Present* of 1977 in Lucerne or *Sentimental Journey* 1979 in Amsterdam… Those are just two possibilities.

"And you? How do you envision the whole thing?

"All the best, Manon"

The filmmaker sent me to watch his movie about the French deconstructivist to show me how we could proceed because he thinks that the philosopher Derrida felt the same kind of resistance that I do and that's exactly what should be addressed in the film. So far so good.

But to my mind, it still wasn't a good film. I don't think the crew had any ambitions at all regarding form, lighting, framing, and even dramaturgy; they just wanted to shoot pure documentary and it made me realize that there's one thing I am absolutely sure about: That is not the way I see "our" film!

We're sitting in the sun in the garden of a small restaurant, almost like a winter resort. The filmmaker is in a good mood as usual, never insulted, receptive, friendly. Our conversation turns out to be surprisingly positive; I feel elated for the first time. He actually seems to understand me a little bit.

Yes, I think we'll take a stab at it.

5 March
Fresh snow. With a double trail already, in front of ours: a big man with a big dog, looks like the dog took the lead.

The locale in the park is well heated, snow all around, the view pure magic. Lots of dogs with their owners, as usual. People say hello to each other.

I make a mental note—which I do occasionally—of all the new things that have conspicuously improved the quality of my personal life in recent years. They are countless. In any case, one of them is this new glass pavilion in the park. Where else could you sit outside in the winter sun to drink your morning coffee with a view of the lake and trees?
    Indispensable, the computer of course, and there's no point in hiding the fact that I've never taken a course. I envy children who grow up with them. I certainly wouldn't be jotting down these notes every day without one, and the inventor of search machines is a genius. And

there's no way you can do without all the other possibilities either. First thing I do in the morning, like everybody else, is start up the computer. But when there's a problem, I have to rely on my husband... He isn't thrilled about that.

Add to that the digital camera that I've had for a couple of years, a mini miracle. I'm almost glad it wasn't around when I was young because taking photos has become so easy that I'd probably accumulate way too many.

Besides, there's no more developing to be done, or agonizing over contact sheets with a magnifying glass. Nobody even remembers that anymore.

Then there's the scooter: my favorite means of daily transport from spring to late fall, and so much fun! For my little dog who had heart trouble—she has since died—I had a little box screwed onto the deck. She loved sitting in it and it meant I could always take her along. We were a hit in the neighborhood.

One of the most important changes for me was a sauna that opened up right at the water directly across from our building.

Not because of the sauna, I didn't use it that much, but because it meant that the beach was open all through the winter from 7 o'clock

in the morning until late at night. Since I became a member, a quick walk across the street
has practically turned into a daily habit. Usually wearing a white terrycloth robe, newspaper
under my arm, to drink my second cup of coffee
on the terrace looking at the waves, followed
by a dip with the divers and sometimes even
a few strokes in the ice-cold lake. My body is
boiling hot afterwards, my heart beating up
to my neck, and I feel gloriously at home in my
body from head to foot. Sometimes at night
just before they close, at 10 o'clock after a
hectic day, a quick dip after work and all the
tension is washed away.

Last year I appropriated the baths, settled down in one of the wooden stalls with a
flashlight, a blanket, bath towels, I even hung
up a mirror, the upper terrace to the far right
belonged to me alone. It was my personal
winter garden.

Now, you're not allowed in anymore.

But "my" stall has become a favorite for a
lot of women. Thanks to the mirror.

Voilá, back to my list of new things:

I think it's almost complete. But I'm sure
there are more delightful things to come. I'm
curious and will love using them.

Oh, the cell phone.

Reminds me of a funny little anecdote that my grandmother, a young farm wife, told me herself about when their telephone was first installed. That was a long time ago. When it rang, she said, Oh, I have to take my apron off first.

Surprisingly, this practical thing is not one of the devices that made a big change in my life. Hardly anybody has my number because I don't want to be called when I'm not at home. It came too late for me. I could have used it a while ago, desperately, when I was suffering from withdrawal symptoms, claustrophobia and agoraphobia, afraid to cross a square, afraid to use public transport, at first I was even afraid to walk a block away from the house. Even afraid of being afraid, it would have been really useful to be able to call a taxi or my husband at any time.

But anxieties are stubborn. They are an issue in all phases of life.

I remember years ago: the Burghölzli clinic. My GP drove me there directly for admission —personally, in his own car.

For sleep therapy.

The observation room is called "Wachsaal" in German. "Wach" means awake—the irony.

Someday in the distant future if I ever have a space large enough at my disposal, I'll design an installation and call it "Wachsaal." My memory of that room is crystal clear, and the way they finally assigned me to a little niche on the side to sleep in. Of course, it'll probably be transformed in the installation.

6 March
Even more snow. The same tracks in the morning, big man, big dog.

Yesterday the exhibition of this artist that everybody admires, the one in the French-speaking part of Switzerland that I had such a loving relationship with. An installation.
Too much, too much. Just too much of everything. A totally masculine show, he laid it on thick.
It didn't move me.
Photographers crowd around him, everybody wants to get a picture of him, preferably with me.
Incidentally, the preceding work, pompous neon installation, very impressive, very big, very expensive, left me cold.

That is not what I want from art.

It's formalism.

I want commitment.

But I do see photographs of other works on my bulletin board that I love more than any-thing, and I like their maker anyway.

At Bellevueplatz today, a pigeon black as a raven as if dressed in mourning. Lately, these pigeons have been decked out in particularly pretty garb. One a perfect Coco Chanel, an-other that I always run into along the quay wears a mauve colored cape. Then there are dark pigeons with snow-white tail feathers and others that wear tweed. And not all of them have symmetrical patterns, as one might think. One of them in dark gray has one wing with radiant white trim and the other a solid gray. I suspect a few thoroughbreds have chosen freedom and are now cheerfully mating with our gray urbanites. It makes for wonderful combinations.

Took a picture of a seagull that's been left with only one leg; its balance hasn't suffered.

How happy I am about this connection to everything that's alive.

There are so many things I used to overlook.

They're coming to pick up the old cat tonight. I'm going to miss her a little. It was fun to see how quickly she trusted us and fit in with our routine.

Aging: I was no doubt the most conspicuous attendee at the recent panel discussion among people who are not exactly at a loss for vanity, me included, and the subject of many photographs.

There was this enchanting, totally unselfconscious young girl in the audience.
    I was never that enchanting, that unselfconscious.

Conversation with a journalist my age who doesn't like women. She doesn't realize that she's debasing herself that way.

An artist from Zurich who I know looks at me and says, "You're as beautiful as ever," at which point his wife knocks her soup all over her dress, the table, and into her handbag. Not even Renée Zellweger in *Bridget Jones's Diary* can beat that.
    The longing for tenderness is even greater than the longing for sex. Was it always like that?

Subjected my husband to a feminist tirade at breakfast this morning because of an article in the paper today. Just can't help myself sometimes: Why men think they are better off marrying the most beautiful instead of the most intelligent women, why women in turn gild themselves with successful or wealthy or famous men, why men don't want to be on par with their partners, preferring the boss's secretary instead, why women, under the circumstances, have no desire to seize a bit of power and influence, what the hell for, why women have such a low opinion of themselves after they have internalized the male gaze without seeing through it. People prefer to identify with the "strong" guy. And on and on. My poor partner.

I have always taken what I wanted. "If a man can do it, I can too." Or more precisely: "If men can take so many liberties, I will take even more."

Luckily my personal life is not affected by all that. Besides, I wouldn't know how to live without a man.
    That's the way it is.

Professionally things look a little different: I am convinced that a male artist with a body of work as comprehensive as mine would be better known today. He would've been taken more seriously from the start. In my case, the first thing they saw, which is what men always see, and most probably always will, is the woman and only after that, the work. (It would be so wonderful if there was room for both side by side.) I've known for all these years that I have to become a neuter (like what happened to Meret Oppenheim) for my art to be taken seriously. Except: I'm still not the least bit interested in revoking my femininity; I'm still a woman.

In one of his last essays in 1998, the French sociologist Pierre Bourdieu wrote about male hegemony:

"Women are in a double bind: if they behave like men, they lose their femininity—as men see it and they themselves as well. If they behave like women, they have lost to begin with."

What a sentence! What a sentence! We should read it again and again! Each and every one of us.
But then: What now? What next?

7 March
Dentist. "Mordre la vie à pleine dents," as the French say.

An interview—magnificent!—on TV with former French Minister of Defense François Léotard, just over 60 years old, living in Fréjus, who voluntarily retired from politics. (In France you can get pretty old in office!)

The interviewer is clearly at a loss. You can tell.

He saw through the mechanism, says Léotard, of this male addiction to power and influence, how life goes astray. *Le bas-fond*, the lowest level at which politicians operate is pretty dark, you kill me, I kill you.

What kind of life is that, he asked himself, where you forget the seasons, don't hear the birds chirping, pay no attention to your garden, have no time to listen to music or read all those books that you would be interested in. It is so much more precious to him today to take a walk along the river with his dogs, the contemplation, just "to be." I remember photographs in *Paris Match*, taken the day after he was elected: Léotard hurrying around the corner in pajamas and slippers to buy croissants and a newspaper as he probably always did. Forgetting that now a dozen photographers would be lying in wait.
That man always appealed to me!

My husband's life fell apart nine years ago yesterday. An elderly woman slammed into his car from behind. He is still suffering from whiplash. "It destroyed my life," he said yesterday during our evening walk; that's the very first time I have ever heard him utter a sentence like that. And I can't think of anyone who has ultimately extracted so much positivity from such a negative event. Since he couldn't work at his old profession anymore, he got another job and started studying on top of it, getting a degree in no time flat. All that's left is his dissertation.

And so both of us, each on our own, are busy working for the future although we are "in middle age," as we call it since he's quite a bit younger than I am. I'm working on new exhibitions and a book; he's working where possible on his dissertation. Makes no difference to me. I'd be just as happy if he were a gardener or a cook. People who do well with plants and animals, who can cook, are sensual. He's an excellent cook by the way.

8 March

It's snowing.

We weighed all of us today. The French bitch weighs almost 6 pounds more than she did in the animal shelter in Paris. That's too much.

Slender dogs live longer. On the other hand, the young dog weighs so little that I can hold him in one hand. A hand snuggler.

At the moment I also weigh a few pounds more than I want to. Moderation was never my strength.

That winter when I started shooting the "Riminis," I was also rather well-rounded. That's why in the first photographs in early January I'm wearing my tall girlfriend's voluminous fur coats. By the time summer came along, during the heatwave, when it was time for skimpy dresses and bathing suits, and above all the nude photographs, I was my usual slim self again. That's the way it's been year after year.

8 March is Women's Day! Ridiculous! Are we some kind of rare species that requires special attention? You might just as well have a special day for sheep, goats, or llamas. But it is revealing because as long as there's no Men's Day, something is not right between the sexes.

There are quite a few things I would wish for men. Such conformists with their hierarchical mentality. I wish they could break out of the rigidity of their self-imposed mold: to be successful, strong, superior, always coping, and good earners on top of it all. Warriors, fighters, conquerors.

That's not the life I want, that's for sure.
 I write letters to the editor.

9 March
Yesterday at the tram stop in the midst of a bustling crowd, a sick or injured pigeon, unable to dodge unsuspecting feet. What was I supposed to do? If I'd had a box, I could've taken it to the vet. But ours, a nice guy from Eastern Europe, would have burst out laughing. He's seen emergencies of a different order in his life.

I just snuck away with a guilty conscience.
 When I got there today, it was gone.

At home I set myself the following task: finally, tabula rasa, which means straightening up the big red table I work at. And that means sorting and putting away all the sketches and notes and drawings for all kinds of projects—piles of paper accumulated from potential installations, photo series, and a host of other possible and impossible ideas. To make room for the two projects I have on my plate. I can't really get down to work until the table is cleared. I can't keep mulling them over in my head forever.

In the process I find notes on stuff I should have taken care of ages ago, like a long overdue visit to the municipal building where Picasso prints are on view at the moment. My publisher wants to organize an exhibition of my work there. I'd completely forgotten about it.

There is a piece of furniture in the basement of my studio, taller than me, with 40 drawers for A4 paper. With labels like: Pending. To do. Urgent!

So far so good. But then:

>   Dead dogs.
>   Hypochondria.
>   The twins.
>   A century of sleep!
>   Installation dancing bear.
>   Ambulance service.
>   A man's world.
>   Absolutely.
>   Petite fleur.
>   The Russian dancer.
>   Bav—book (?).
>   M.e. (?).

As well as:

>   Stamped designs.
>   Costume designs.
>   Books of ideas.

Or:

Titles.
Sentences.
Texts.
Ideas for shows.
Environments.
Performances.
Objects.

Work sketches disappear into drawers with such labels, usually forever; there they stay, forgotten. Because ninety percent of the ideas never materialize. On top of that, there are these brown boxes, at least a dozen, that serve the same purpose. They're stuffed full, have been for years, probably never to be looked through again.

10 March
The snow in front of the house is gone, I almost regret it, but the hills opposite are still white. The first rays of sun already appear at eight in the morning. Three ducks are flying along the shore. Followed by five seagulls in formation, and the first sparrow is at my feeder. Spring starts officially on 21 March.

In the park a minute ago this overwhelming feeling of happiness again. Birds chirping in trees and hedges, and the owl that's already been hooting for days. My Parisian is suddenly carried away, full of life, racing around the meadow in circles, with the young dog hard on her heels.

Every day I gaze up at the slowly growing crows' nest. I've since discovered a second one, so beautifully camouflaged you can barely see it. When I watch the creatures flying from treetop to treetop, I feel like a bird myself for a second as if I were floating. Then, there's not a single question left open.
Everything is as it is.

With astonishment, I note that my winter depression has chosen not to plague me this year. In fact, is this maybe the happiest time of my life?
If I had known earlier: beauty fades but happiness increases.

There it is again: the inner peace that was so alien to me for so many years.

Could you perhaps also call it love? Love of everything that's alive.

A couple of years ago I learned to cultivate little sources of well-being, ones that don't rely on other people. Books, the sight of the water, nature, the company of animals.

Animals can take the edge off a difficult life.

I used to be so restless I kept changing lovers all the time, in rapid succession. I had to conquer any man who was unusual in some way and therefore appealed to me. Later, when AIDS became an issue, and I was newly married to this extremely special man—and still am—I kept changing cities instead, and still later apartments (with him). Even here in the same Frascati building, we moved from the first floor up to the second, and then back again to the first, but to a different apartment. This time in the curve of the house where my big bed is framed by two voluptuous trees in front of the window.
　　Which is where I wanted to be to begin with.

It feels as if I've spent my life running away. Hounded. Breathless.

They're burying Elena F. today.
　　I won't be there, we were never close. Her son moved in with me shortly after he graduated from high school.

His first name was Hans. I instantly called him Salamander because he was so many different people.

I still call him that, to this day.

We spent the wildest years together. Seven all told. And I'd do it again. Except for that bit at the end, the drugs—better change the subject.

My father's funeral, and my mother's, too, a few years earlier—can barely remember them, I've never visited the graves.

But I do remember my youngest sister being there, her face a pallid yellow. I knew she wouldn't live long.

Before she passed, she supposedly said, "It's hard to die." She was still so young.

Sometimes I think if she managed, I can too, later, later, someday when the time comes.

My father said his wife killed herself with the help of medication. She had sent him away and when he came back she was dead.

I might have done that, too, in her place.

They never investigated.

I remember her standing in the bedroom—I was still a child—in front of the open closet door and putting on a pink slip. Then she put the tip of her foot under the double bed and slowly started massaging her right leg, almost tenderly, sliding her hands from bottom to top, then the left leg.

I think she loved her body.

She was considered a beautiful woman.

The pigeons again, what should I do? Is it because these polymorphic urbanites have recently begun slipping through the filter of my perception? An entire miniature universe! And I missed it!

Some people supposedly hate pigeons.

I'm so happy to share the city with other living creatures.

I was totally engrossed in the sight of plumage so eccentric that Picasso would have loved it. I was trying to memorize the design so that I could describe it later.

Then an ambulance raced by sirens screaming and the bird vanished. Later an announcement: accident (they call it collision) at Wiedikon station. Exactly where I'd been five minutes before. They rerouted the trams. I could feel my heart beating in my neck: I was scared! Scared about what might've happened to somebody. I heard a woman behind me say, "She had more luck than brains." What a relief. I started breathing again.

It's a sad and a beautiful world.

About two years ago I took the plunge, decided to fight my anxiety about accidents, illness, and death by buying a decommissioned ambulance, an especially beautiful model, a cream-colored Mercedes, and totally revamping the interior. Covered it with sugar-candy colored fleece like a cocoon and made it as intimate as the inside of a seashell. With Chanel N°5 in the IV.
   The students and teachers of a textile class gave me practical help.

Manon's Ambulance Service has since been in storage at an art museum waiting for its next performance. The last time, it was on display for a relatively long event in front of that same museum in the midst of winter, after the museum director had completely overhauled it. My husband drove especially to St. Gallen to take a picture of it. The ambulance, radiating a luminous bright pink in the white snow. A lovely image.

Its predecessor was an ambulance on the streets of Paris. They told me a beautiful prostitute had settled down in it. I found my-self gazing at every single ambulance passing by, fantasizing about countless interiors.

Both Zurich dailies, the *NZZ* and the *Tages-Anzeiger*, published my letter to the editor including my title: "Women, a Rare Species?"

Received an invitation to an exhibition in Switzerland's capital. They screened the only video I've ever made. It's called: *Focus Switzerland. Video Art since 1970*. How poetic.

11 March
Early in the morning, when the sun behind our building just reaches the horizon, it bathes the row of buildings on the other side of the lake in gold for a moment, almost like a shimmer-ing necklace.
    You can see the first buds up in the treetops; the branches down below are still bald.

But the sky was so incredibly red tonight that it looked like the lake was reflecting blood.

"Every old man was once young, but not every young man gets old." I read that somewhere recently.

Well, one of the issues I'm supposed to be thinking about is what it feels like when the beauty of youth slowly fades. So I ask myself about the people in my life, how they're doing, and how they feel about getting older with me.

The first of my three husbands—I was still a minor and had to get my parents' written permission—is practically the same age as I am and has become a handsome, gray-haired man. I learned a lot from this early love and he knows that he can depend on me for the rest of his life.

Whenever I have marriage woes or other troubles, I run to him. He puts me down on the couch, covers me, and I cry my eyes out. I can only do that with him. Then he turns on the radio, Swiss jazz, and begins cooking for us in the kitchen. Everything is easier after that.

He was a womanizer, but I didn't actually realize it until after I'd left him. We talk a lot about getting old nowadays. He calls himself a fatalist, but when I stop by unannounced, I sometimes catch him doing exercises. Besides, he knows all about healthy nutrition and is a passionate cyclist; he's still slender and muscular.

My second husband was an exquisitely beautiful artist; the press touted him as a wunderkind and he was pretty famous for a while. To me he was beauty and poetry incarnate. He was barely 20 years old when we met. He had cheated, made himself a couple of years older, for an exhibition at Kunsthaus Zürich and for me. By the time he finally confessed, we were already passionately and symbiotically intertwined.

He soon made a name for himself thanks to his exceptional talent and being photogenic beyond belief, and has since become a man of repute, an art professor in a German city. He looked pretty good on the cover of an art magazine two or three years ago, wearing a black terrycloth bathrobe, head shaved, with an expression of gravity, a man who takes himself seriously, sensuous mouth, pointy ears, like a bat, his firm hand holding the picture of a very beautiful, dark-haired young man, tears streaming down his face. The man in the picture is wearing a snakeskin jacket and a dark silk foulard, white numbers printed on it, made out of a summer dress of mine.

He told me he wanted to look like the actor Edward G. Robinson someday, striking and distinctive. He has succeeded. He deposited his youth and beauty in the checkroom of vanity, too soon, I think; he could have put it off a bit longer but maybe it was a wise decision. The last time he stopped by in my city, he told me about a heart attack and I sensed what an invasive event it must have been. I mention that here because his new work refers to it.

Even though our relationship—it felt like Siamese twins—ultimately had to end, the severance was painful. I still feel empathy and affection for him, and always will.

But then I was free!
Free. Free. Free.
I had nothing left to lose!
I could dare to do anything,
step across boundaries,
risk everything!

The foundation was laid for my first appearance on the art scene, which ultimately caused an uproar and paved the way for my actual life, my own life.

Later the Salamander became part of my existence and my soulmate for life, though it has quieted down. He still has his curls but they're gray now. "The new man in Manon's life is a poet," the gossip column opined. Well, the distinguished young charmer—my girlfriend called him lover boy—has also become a man.

His appearance deliberately understated as opposed to his eccentric youth, he has still retained his own distinctive style, his boyish behavior, infectious enthusiasm, and incisive mind. Maybe he will never really grow up, that's fine by me. He has abandoned the wild life, like all of us who survived. But his mind is as wild as ever. Thank God.

A loyal fatherly admirer, all my life. He made a Manon out of his last girlfriend—a pretty well-known writer—because he was obsessed with my looks and basically, she was too. He died, whereupon the writer, who fell ill shortly afterwards, took her life with the help of an assisted suicide organization. The press wallowed in the story for weeks.

He was the only man in my life who was several years older than me, but athletic, fit, and in great shape. He was only forty when we met but already had white hair, and he was vain, spoiled, and demanding. Always impeccably dressed thanks to tailors in Milan and London—much too perfect for my taste. I always missed just a tiny touch of negligence.

He was the one who taught me that cashmere is softer than wool, sable more valuable than mink, silk more sensuous than cotton, and Bal à Versailles the best perfume in the world.

No matter where I was, I could always call him and he would be there, regardless of who I happened to be with at the moment.

Though I didn't take much advantage of that possibility.

He's been dead for quite a while now. Our last encounter: he and the writer showed up at our doorstep—we were already living in the Frascati House—out of the blue. He seemed a little fragile, and they were each holding a burning candle.

It was shortly before Christmas.

The tender, blonde youth, a brand-new graduate, who I went to Paris with and who co-authored the photographs that have since become so well-known—which is why he is mentioned in my first monograph—did not turn into a happy man. Extremely sensitive, vulnerable, and difficult, with unconditional faith in my faculties, he also suffered because of that and finally left me.

In his foreword to my first little book, he wrote about how we traveled abroad together: *La première fois que j'ai vu Manon, je l'ai prise pour une stripteaseuse dans son jour de sortie.* [The first time I saw Manon I thought she was a striptease artist on her day off.]

When I traveled to the seaside by train last winter with three dogs, he came along to help me change trains and then took the train home again. That's not something to be taken for granted. We hadn't seen one another for a long time; he thought I hadn't changed. I felt exactly the same way about him. We took up the conversation right where we had left off years earlier.

That wasn't the issue.

In Paris, *le stil du pauvre* is what they call a certain kind of elegance based on imagination instead of money. He cultivated it, brilliantly, as he always had, and for a couple of years we shared the same style.

Let me add the French-speaking artist who meant something, in fact a lot, to me, when I was back in Switzerland. I saw him recently. At his last show in my city, a woman standing behind me in the audience said, "He's still cute."

Not to forget my artist friend, both draftsman and photographer: when we met, neither of us played a role in the art scene yet. I had gone up to him on the street and told him how much I had always noticed him. We've been friends ever since.

Today, after many lows, he is considered one of the most important photographers; the French TV anchor Frédéric Mitterrand called him, "le plus grand photographe de garçon du monde." His face resembles Henry Miller's, so how can anything go wrong? At least once a year, usually twice, he goes on a fasting diet and follows a strict daily schedule: swimming pool, healthy whole foods, no alcohol, no all-nighters. His performances, you can certainly call them that when he appears at public events, are meticulously composed. Unadulterated discipline. We admire him for that.

And his love life?

He says he's not so good at that.

But my beautiful, much beloved girlfriend, a well-known publisher's reader who has stood by me in more than a few crises, striking, tall, blonde, carrying a white Pekingese à la Jean Harlow—no one could have looked better— multitudes of men secretly doting on her, went to the other side. The side where vanity's not an issue anymore. And at a point when other people are just getting their second wind.

I haven't succeeded in following suit yet and, to be honest, I resented her for doing that because outwardly there was nothing left of the woman who had once appealed to me so much. Life is apparently pretty comfortable on the other side and maybe we'll meet up there someday, maybe even pretty soon.

Not like our girlfriend in Paris, Helmut Newton's photo model and a mini celebrity, familiar to God and the world, from the most intimate of perspectives and whose existence revolved exclusively around eroticism or, to be more precise, sexuality. Not a single man who didn't desire her, not a single man that she didn't seduce. Everything is just like it used to be, the apartment, the snakelike clothing, the page-boy haircut, the behavior, except that this sex bomb, this slender and yet curvaceous young girl—I have never seen a more beautiful female body—has now become a typical French maman. The wittiest, funniest woman I know. "C'est quelqu'un," as the French say.

An authority. She still spoils her guests with the best cuisine in Paris. She's famous for her *dîners* too, though possibly no longer crowned with erotic desserts.
No one knew exactly what she lived on but she was and is well acquainted with prominent men in politics and show business, was invited by important bankers, had affairs with famous pop stars and other artists, and led an exciting

life. She has since written a book about it; I read the first draft in a single go. I hope it gets published because she writes well, exactly the way she lives and talks: totally point-blank.

I can't list my third husband here as an example because, even though he's a tiny bit gray at the temples, he's simply still too young. "The marriage nobody believed in has already lasted seven years," wrote a well-known people journalist quite a few years ago. Well, it's lasted and lasted, who would've thought so, and it's become utterly indispensable. Through all these years, my partner has never, ever left me high and dry, not one single time, no matter what the problem was, and there have been many—still are.

Incidentally, a few years ago a well-known and popular press photographer—his entire archive burned to the ground in the old town a while ago—managed to get a picture of me at an art opening with all three husbands.

Captured the decisive moment...

Proved a pretty photograph: the artist in the middle, obviously the focal point of the group, in a dark suit and white shirt, shaved head, coat over his arm, holding a wine glass. Penetrating, curious gaze, a little skeptical, too, as he looks to the right at my current husband: short black hair, black eyes, black coat, attractive and young, looking at the camera with what you might almost describe as a slightly malicious smile. I'm standing to the left of the artist, facing him, raccoon coat (shame on me), hair down, gazing at the focal point of the photograph, namely, the artist. And next to him, the oldest one in the group, the only one totally relaxed, radiant, hands in his pants pockets, light-colored clothing, casual, but groomed for the event. He's the only one looking out into space. Almost an historic document, at least for me.

Thank you, dear Niklaus Stauss.

12 March

This morning is the first time in ages that looks exactly like a typical gloomy winter day: gray in gray, neither sun nor snow, the ground frozen.

I want to lay a trail—like Hansel and Gretel did to find their way home—by hanging nuggets of bird food on trees, starting with the one in front of my house until all the way to the end of the park. Later they'll be covered by the delicate green of spring and only I will know where they are.

In the trees behind my bed, in the bay window of my bedroom, the buds are discreetly making their first appearance. You have to look really hard to see them.

Taking a night walk along the lake, saw someone rummaging around with a bunch of plastic bags, behind the construction fence, where about 50 swans spend the night. It's too dark to tell, but I know who it is. Mrs. Bölsterli, that reliable, faithful soul, year after year, month after month, day after day, you see her with her cart full of old bread going to several specific spots to feed the swans. She goes to the neighborhood bakery every morning to get the old rolls from the day before. And all this time, there's only been one interruption when she was in the hospital with cancer. That was a couple of years ago. Not even the subsequent radiation and chemotherapy stopped her. After that, she walked with a cane for a while and looked a little haggard. She can tell most of her animals apart, which ones are males, which ones females, whether they are young or old. She's even named some of them, knows their life histories. If one of them is sick or injured, she gets help from the lake police. Apparently, there are certain swans she can even hold in her arms.

They say she was an opera singer. Under her little plastic hat full of seagull droppings, you can sense a pretty, delicate face. Sometimes I meet her when I go shopping and we talk about my dogs or about her deceased cat.

I have yet to establish a personal relationship with these long-necked creatures. But I did manage to feed the swans regularly in France, in a nature reserve where my husband and I usually anchor our houseboat. One summer a pitch-black swan came swimming toward us in the midst of a group of white ones. A miracle. None of the animals that stop by every day seems to think there's anything odd about that.
But the following summer it was gone.

On the other hand, half on its side, its neck forming a graceful line on its body, we see a dead swan floating in the middle of the sluggish river. The defenselessness, the abandonment of the pose moved me deeply.

I take pictures of him at different times to record the stages of decay.

Only then does it occur to me that I have never seen a dead animal in the waters of my town, neither a swan nor a seagull nor a duck. I wonder if the animals go ashore to die. Or whether they collect the bodies in the morning before the first fishermen or joggers are out.

Bellinzona 1977. *Seduzione e dolore*, seduction and pain, is what I called my first installation, featuring three swans, two females and one male with impressively spread wings, along with five two-sided, standing mirrors, revolving on their own axis as if ceaselessly dancing with themselves. It was about vanity, about beauty, about transience. What better animal to represent these eternal issues?

13 March
For the first time this year, on an unexpectedly sunny, warm day, a whole hoard of people came trundling past our house on their way down to the park at the lake. I love that. Vacation atmosphere. The restaurant under my terrace has set the tables up outside and they're all full. Now it's back again, the backdrop of summer sounds that I prefer above all others.

There's murmuring, soft laughter, transistor radios from time to time, cheerful people. It's so wonderful to be alone in my apartment with the balcony doors wide open, in the midst of so much life. How I miss that in winter!

Occasionally, actually rarely, people glance up at our house and discover that people live there.

Since my sister died, still so very young, I can't help myself, year after year the same anxious question: And what if this is my last spring?

How many of the people who have accompanied my life for a shorter or longer time, close by or far away, are already gone? There's been illness, drugs, suicide.

Politics!

Fattebert! Never will men understand why such a "minor" verbal faux pas like that of the French-speaking SVP Congressman, who said, in reference to the inaugural address of the new President of the Council, in other words, the highest office in Switzerland, "Nobody is without mistakes and she's excused because she's a woman." ...that is quite simply inexcusable. The condescension, the arrogance!

Just imagine the situation in reverse! And people wonder why women don't try to grab positions of that kind. There's not much to gain but plenty to lose, namely dignity.

It makes me just plain livid that men like Fattebert are utterly incapable of getting the point. These are our politicians and ultimately there is nothing that is not influenced by their humiliating attitudes: the economy, society, families. As long as men occupy positions of power, nothing will ever change because they don't even notice that there is a gender issue. It is so disheartening.

Once again I resort to a letter to the editor. What else can I do?

Recently, Swiss TV asked me to take part in a program about beauty. Instead I sent the editor an email telling her that I would rather she address the above-mentioned issue.

That will take a while.

Oh, let's just drop it.

14 March
Today, after going to the doctor and having a cup of morning coffee at Café Odeon afterwards, I plan to stop at a photo booth. To compare, to keep using the same medium to document the passage of time. Those machines are not objective because they use a flash, which inevitably makes the pictures look "flatter." That's, incidentally, why the photographs in gossip columns are usually so flatering.

There is probably hardly anyone of my generation who doesn't have dozens of photo strips. A few insider tips about these booths: some of them, specifically older models, have very sharp focus and my artist friend from Zurich told me about two of them. They're out of the way, though, since we moved so I'll use one of those that have the advantage of being able to look at yourself first and perfect your pose before taking the picture. And if you don't like it, you can even do it over again.

So, no health problems and I've got the pictures. In color. To be dated and put away in a file that also contains the very first series in black-and-white when I was 18 and still had dimples. It's fascinating to trace how you change over the years. It isn't shocking. Although I did make myself especially pretty today, I owe it to myself.

There are quite a few pairs in the filed photographs, too, me with my respective partner, as we all know, and also with simultaneous or shorter affairs, that I won't mention here even though not a single one was unimportant.

So in the first photographs, I'm with the beautiful artist, the one who's so photogenic it takes your breath away. The mouth, the shadows on the cheeks, the dark eyes. The light skin, shoulder length black hair, parted on the side. Often wearing sunglasses more as an accessory than because of the sun, or the tip of a cigarette dangling between his lips. He resembles the eccentric French film actor Pierre Clémenti, who we both incidentally idolized, and whose acquaintance I later made in Paris.

Actually I should insert another photograph between the one above and the next one, a photograph of the young man who lived with me a short while, incredibly attractive, in a completely different, "wilder" way, who went back to South America where his mother came from years ago and still contacts me regularly, having found me on the Internet. I couldn't resist his look; I'm not sure if he was really in love with me even if he insists on believing it.

I think he was more in love with his image of me. In any case, I was certainly taken with him and could not resist his erotic aura.

He happened to be the son of an actor; the German TV series was called *Graf Yoster gibt sich die Ehre* (Count Yoster makes an appearance).

And he gave me my first cat! The Siamese.

Next, the first picture with the Salamander: head of wild, dark curly hair, pointed chin, lips so enchantingly outlined that even men succumbed to them. Black velvet jacket, nipped in at the waist, and underneath a glittering silver, wide V-neck top.

He looks pretty wasted in later photographs.

At different points there are also pictures with my fatherly admirer, the beautifully tanned dandy because he goes skiing in St. Moritz and anchors his yacht at the Costa Smeralda. He's hiding behind me but his gesture is very loving, you might in fact say almost devoted.

In one of the strips I'm wearing a roomy, dark brown mink coat, exactly the same color as my hair, but I never really felt it belonged to me. It was meant as consolation after my second husband and I had separated and I was extremely sad.

The fur coat was stolen shortly afterwards in Venice.
    It was such a relief!

The photographs that follow are with my multi-talented artist friend from Zurich. He looks good, lush blonde hair, radiant smile, eyes just narrow slits, almost the way he looks today, just younger. A lot younger.

Later, the first picture with "my" student, before we went to Paris: bright face, delicate features, the most conspicuous feature his huge, very dark eyes under beautiful eyebrows, bushy blonde hair, down to his chin, a cigarillo in his mouth. He is wearing a black jacket, too, with pointy shoulders, and a wide open white shirt with a white foulard. There is something slightly decadent about him and at the same time he seems a little lost.

Then I discover a picture of a very young girlfriend with long red hair. She cooked for me, comforted and admired me after the student had left me. She's placed a protecting arm over my shoulders. We're a rather odd couple: she, very tall, very young, very natural, and me, daintier, quite a bit older, and glamorous. Much later, she married my first husband. Sadly I don't have any photo strips of him or with him. Said marriage didn't last.

Soon afterwards the first pictures with my current husband crop up. His hair, matchstick length, still coal black, well-tanned, aristocratic nose, beautiful teeth.

We are gazing at one another enraptured. This is the first time a dog makes an appearance, a small one. I'm no longer as young as I used to be. You can tell this woman has been through a lot and probably didn't pamper herself.

Then, no more pictures for seven years.

I've learned, from Salamander's daughter, that today's teenagers are crazy about these photo booths despite digital photography and cell phones. You gradually get to know yourself a little better that way, and you also get to know how you're seen from outside.

Will that ever end, will there ever be a time when people no longer want to look at themselves or compare?

I've been making these notes for three weeks now and filled almost 27 pages, that makes at least one page a day on average. If I keep it up, it would amount to more than 365 pages by the end of the year.

I am so glad that my life has quieted down. There was a time when it would've been absolutely impossible to write regular entries on top of everything else.

Shortly after my monograph was published, the author, she later killed herself, suggested writing my biography as well. I wasn't ready yet.

But two or three years ago, when a young journalist, I already mentioned her, had the same idea, but an entirely different concept, I sat down at the computer to draft thoughts all by myself on what I could tell her about my life as an artist and a woman. The writing came easily to me, without even thinking about it, the text practically flowed out of my "pen." These chapters must be somewhere in the mysterious depths of my computer, no idea where that might be, because from one moment to the next, I had to put an end to the entire thing: the egomania! As I recall, I got as far as the chapter titled "Seven Wild Years."

I left that chapter out, instead continuing with my years in Paris and then back to Zurich via Geneva.

"Manonomania" is how the Salamander described the way certain people relate to me, and probably also the way I relate to myself. In any case, that's what I called one of my "artist books," I call them my "black books." Egomania or Manonomania, regardless, I suddenly had the feeling that the word "I" was much too dominant. Now the same feeling washes over me as I skim through these notes before sending them (uncensored!) to the filmmaker as we agreed so that he has something to get his teeth into.

And not only that: I feel terribly embarrassed.

That's going to be an obstacle to further writing.

15 March
But giving up is not an option.

Every morning I walk the dogs, alone or with my partner, along the lake in one direction or the other, depending on the time of year and the weather. You often run into the same people, mostly fellow dog lovers. At some point I notice a new daily walker I've never seen before: a large, imposing gentleman with shoulder length white hair, a beautiful slender head, he must've been extremely handsome once. He walks erect, wears fine clothing, matching colors. I guess advertising, graphic arts, art dealer. But there are discrepancies.

He looks at the ground, never takes note of the lake or the trees. A discreet scruffiness betrays him, he has suddenly lost his job. His presence has become a daily habit and something is missing when he isn't there. One day I start saying hello to him. Sometimes he responds, sometimes he doesn't. Several times I try to start a conversation—in vain. But we do wish each other Merry Christmas and later a Happy New Year. It's been like that for two or three years, he never even glances at his surroundings, he could just as well be walking along a railroad track. He's here again today, wearing the same clothes, shabbier now, his hair is longer, unwashed, and he has grown a beard. But more noticeable than anything else is the way he walks. It has changed, he takes smaller steps, his shoulders hunched, as if he were collapsing in on himself.

Sometimes I thought I should invite him for a cup of coffee, but then, what next? Would he or would I feel obliged to pursue this curious relationship? It would be complicated.

We leave it as it is.

Now that the temperature is going up and it's almost unusually warm, the time has come. It's been in the air for the past couple of days: my partner is sick and so am I, again. The flu is going around. He is lying in his room, I'm in mine, with doors open on both sides. Whereby his bedroom is more accessible than mine, which adjoins my work space.

And we both have important appointments. The Parisian sticks to him, the young dog to me. The cats take turns.

16 March
Pre-spring.

Although still under the weather, I take an early morning walk along the lake, all the way to the front where I can sit on stone stairs and the view is wide open. I want to see the mountains. And take pictures. I would never have dreamed of doing that earlier! I was primarily interested in exceptional, unusual things.

What a pity!

The park has lost some of its unruliness. Most of it was flattened out this winter, all that's left is grass and trees, practically not a single bush or shrub. Every single drug hideout has been eliminated. Even though the only thing North Africans sell—and I know this for a fact—is hash and in the first bend at the entrance to the park.

When I go to the park at night, I feel safe when they're around.

A small step across the quay in the afternoon to see how renovations of the bathing area are coming along. Two old wading pools will be covered with wooden planks to be used for sunbathing. Children stopped coming here ages ago and the sauna is getting a steam bath and new showers.

I have a memory of the beach from long, long ago. I had just left my first husband for an actor (he had a profile like the young Marlon Brando and was very talented). I was a student myself at this academy, I hadn't met my second husband yet and was not a happy person and not yet an artist. The memory is so fresh it could have been yesterday. Both the future actor and my fatherly admirer were out of town. I loved it because I felt completely free. I went to the beach late in the afternoon, to the upper terrace, to the far right, the one for old women, lay down on the wooden slats in between old-fashioned bathing suits and sunburnt, blotchy skin with the smell of suntan lotion, and watched the clouds. Happiness just washed over me, a very rare feeling, and I had just one desire: to have this terrace all to myself and all year-round.

Those were three weeks of unmitigated bliss.

Petite Fleur, which opened seven years ago as the first official and most renowned brothel in our city, is being forced to close down. It's being auctioned off mid-April. A year ago I had the idea of taking pictures of all 30 rooms in the building, extremely distinctive both in view of size and subject matter, because the prostitutes rent them and can furnish them as they please. Rooms have always fascinated me, and I wanted to know to what extent the tenants give their rooms a personal touch, whether there are little still lifes, trinkets, stuffed animals, photographs, or whether they remain relatively prosaic, geared only to their profession. I was curious and wanted to take a look behind scenes that are ordinarily off limits for women. I thought I might even be able to produce a small publication. And then I had the idea of renting a room myself for a while (CHF 200 per day or rather night) to get a close-up view of the operations, but also because the rooms are free at such different times.

Today I realize that the owner had his own worries without having to deal with some photo artist, although he was basically open to the project and even knew my work—which I certainly hadn't expected. In any case, we never

came to an agreement. The women themselves, largely from Eastern Europe, South
America, and sub-Saharan Africa, were totally
against being photographed, and there were
supposedly illegal prostitutes as well. That's
why the manager was given a suspended
jail sentence.

At our meetings, he was very polite and proved
to be a real family man. He liked talking about
his children and one of them, a daughter, runs
the brothel. When some of the women—very
nice, incidentally, and beautiful—showed me
their rooms, they asked me if I was going
to work there, too. I had to laugh and almost
felt flattered.

As far as the moral aspect of prostitution is
concerned, and by that I don't mean the fact
that women do such work but that they come
here from poor countries in order to do it—
I don't even want to think about it. Because
it's not about morals, it's about politics.

Massive police raid around 8 PM at the entrance to the park. They're after the hash
dealers this time.

17 March

Although we aren't fully recovered yet, my partner and I, we're finally going to the city where I went to school as a child to check out the building that's earmarked for an exhibition.

The filmmaker is sitting at his desk, in Berlin, working on an exposé. A lovely picture.

I would like a bittersweet, melancholy, hyper-aesthetic film, a film like an acid trip, yes, exactly like that, a film that pays deliberate, meticulous attention in every single scene to the lighting, the framing, the most beautiful angle. He's a documentary filmmaker and probably wants to film things as is. "Nothing should be changed," he said during a shoot. Changing nothing is what aggravates me most of all; changing things to their advantage is what I can do best of all.

We're going to get into each other's hair. A lot will depend on the cameraman's skills.

And my friend's confession didn't simplify matters, a well-known director I've already worked with, also a documentary filmmaker. She said she had wanted to make this movie, already had this project in mind when she asked me if somebody had beat her to it.

We hugged each other and were very sad because I would have dearly loved to work with her.

That left me confused for a while because I really liked the last film she made about an artist, the one about Dieter Roth, and I also like working with women, always have. All in all, several people had the same idea, the subject seems to be in the air. It looks like I'm the only one who hasn't seen the light, or maybe I'm just wary of it? Afraid I won't measure up to expectations? Expectations of others and my own? Or of a male filmmaker?
Yes, I'm afraid of this film.

18 March
What a pleasure it is to have the windows open when you wake up. Still half-asleep you can tell spring has really come; certain sounds are a dead giveaway.

The exhibition venue in the government building has turned out to be a really good space for my pictures.

"The Late Years of Women Artists." Could have been an interesting topic but the art historian's rhetoric was abominable; we walked out in the middle.

But I did take a photograph of Louise Nevelson's portrait. I was very young when I discovered the sculptor with her monumental, mostly monochrome black or white wooden reliefs in New York and I admired her appearance as much as I did her work. I thought that's exactly what I want to look like when I'm eighty. She wore sumptuous, theatrical clothing, turbans, lavish jewelry, and makeup like an opera diva for the stage. It was so impressive! And in the end, it was also touching because sometimes her false eyelashes were a little crooked and black mascara stuck to her cheek.

There was a place for her, she had already died, in my homage installation *la stanza delle donne* for an exhibition in Genoa, on view before and afterwards in Swiss museums where it was called *Das Damenzimmer* (Room for a Lady). By the way, there's a figure in the MISS RIMINI series, I call it "Actress Before Going on Stage"; holding a blonde wig, her own hair tucked under a stocking, she could have been modeled after Nevelson.

My fantasy about this portrait: the actress was playing the mistress and was afraid it might be her last time.

That's the picture I've chosen for the cover of the book.

In any case, my friend and I ended up spending last night someplace else. I told him about the art dealer who had considered keeping me as his mistress—we were at an extremely expensive Parisian restaurant, in a private room—how he was calculating what the upkeep of a woman like me would cost him, that was how his mind worked, and how that painful incident had recently come back to haunt me. My friend told me that the same man boasts in German newspapers about buying the works of certain artists for next to nothing and selling them for a small fortune in the United States.

Wintercoattime—what a nice word—wintercoattime is over.

A few quick rounds in town with the scooter, holding an enthusiastic Parisian in my left hand. Lots of people smile at us.

Took a walk along the lake with the art teacher. She tells me about her weekend in Germany with a group of nice people and two doctors, daring to try LSD for the first time. Tells me about seeing deep inside herself and how she suddenly understood everything, saw herself in the world and the world in herself, recognizing her longings but also finding a life of her own, a life that suits her. How she didn't just hear music but saw it and how towards the end of her high, outside in the open air, nature embraced her in a wonderful way, enclosing her in a great overarching whole.

That's it; that's exactly it.

The park at night: the North Africans are gone.

19 March
I don't think I've ever seen spring appear so suddenly. No transition. They just predicted snow, freezing temperatures, and now an ice cream vendor at every corner, practically summer temperatures.

The piles on my tables keep getting bigger instead of smaller, notebooks lying all over the place, in handbags, my beach bag, next to, under, and behind the bed. I think I'll try throwing everything into one big heap and patiently start trimming it down, page by page. What I want right now is a big empty space with bare white walls. Where I could sort the "year in snapshots" from last year, hang them up, organize them, get an overview and decide on a sequence. The best thing would be to go to another city, or better yet, another country, where I would have nothing else to deal with.

Supper outside!

20 March

I always leaf through biographies from the back. First thing I want to know is how old people were, how they finally died. There's one passage I remember from the Thursday lecture about the American painter Georgia O'Keeffe. A lot of women idolized her, her archaic way of life, almost completely alone in the Mexican desert at the end of her life. There's a famous, marvelous photograph of her as a very old woman, wearing a severe black dress with a white collar. A beautiful, totally wrinkled face, a gentle smile, her gaze introspective all the way down to her fingertips, tenderly holding, feeling a clay object, maybe a jug. She was almost blind by that time. The art historian tells us that she was eighty years old when she painted her last picture. She was 98 when she died. 18 years in between! How did those years pass, what was her life like?

I take down my big book of her work. The last picture reproduced in it was painted in 1972, she called it *black rock*, painted on a white column against a light blue sky with white clouds. In the chronology it says: 1973–1983, so for 10 years, "traveled to Morocco, Antigua, Guatemala, Costa Rica, and Hawaii with Juan Hamilton."

Juan Hamilton, ceramicist: who was this man, 58 years younger than O'Keeffe, who taught her to make pottery when her eyesight failed and then took these trips with her?

There's practically nothing about that.
Then: "Died 1986 in Santa Fe, New Mexico."
So she lived for 98 years.

They published my letter to the editor in today's newspaper with the headline: "Men Will Never Understand."

In the meantime, others have settled in alongside the ice cream vendors: the hotdog stand in the middle of the park, the musicians, alone or in groups, turtle doves, radiant, totally absorbed in each other, the punks with their dogs and their rats, picnicking families and at night, that's what I like best, down by the lake, the dark men, singing their melancholy songs and dancing, men among themselves. Memories of Paris, the Arab quarter, where nobody could believe that a woman would voluntarily shave off her hair.

Acquaintances have asked me if I make a big detour around all these people. On the contrary, should I? This is life.

21 March

Dinner last night, me and my husband, invited by the friend who helped me put together my first installation, *The Salmon-Colored Boudoir*, a 12-sided mirrored chamber with a canopy. He was fresh out of school and part of a small clique, they were always around, involved in whatever I was doing. He followed my path that led into the art scene and onwards. There is a photograph of him in one of my "black books": this slender young man with life still ahead of him. Black Brylcreemed Mohawk above his pretty face with blue eyes and precise eyebrows, plucked, pretty unusual for somebody in those days who obviously wasn't gay. He's wearing one of those show suit jackets that I used to design and that were pictured in a lot of magazines. "Manon Conquers Paris," or some such headline in any number of languages.

He still has the jacket.

In the meantime, he has become a man of some stature. You can tell that he has lived well.
I'm not the same anymore either.

On the way home I show my husband the house where I lived for two or three years with my first husband. That was a long time ago. I look up at the window and remember what a helpless and desperately unhappy person lived behind it. Not because of my partner but because I had not yet acquired a faculty for happiness. Because I didn't know who I was yet, who I wanted to be, what I needed, what was good for me. Staggering blindly from one day to the next, I saw no future ahead. We hadn't chosen the apartment, it had been offered to us, we rented it sight unseen. I had not yet learned how important the space is that you inhabit and the light and the path that leads to the building, because you have to like walking along it. I knew nothing, nothing at all. Except for one thing, and it was already an imperative when I was little: a room of my own. All my life. (And without having read Virginia Woolf.)

After months in a mental institution, I moved, still a minor, into this nondescript building with my equally young husband. Light from the north-west, a dreary street in front of the window.

I tried to make the best of it anyway:

The room, my room, would be a refuge, I put a round birdcage in the middle. The birds sat on their eggs nonstop. When the eggs hatched, I took the fledglings back to the pet store and the cycle started all over again.

It's hard for me to talk about this, but for a while everything seemed so bleak to me that I stopped eating, I wasn't the least bit hungry and I didn't even see the birds anymore.

When I looked at the cage again, I weighed 83 pounds and the birds were dead. They had starved to death. Just writing this down fills me with horror and makes me feel so ashamed. I don't recognize myself.

Another memory is of an unfortunate dog, a dachshund with floppy ears and long red hair just like mine was at the time, I'm actually a redhead. And the cat, I think it was black. The dog got run over, one of my sisters was looking after him, and the cat didn't fare too well either.

Only later, much later, did I learn to love and live.

Today I'm going to start printing out my "a year of quick pictures." With great reluctance, because the creative, fun work is done. Now it's just a matter of organizing the pictures. Actually, that's not quite true, grouping them to make compelling combinations is just as creative. But my mind is elsewhere, I've moved on and the pictures are from last year.

If the outcome was a book instead of an exhibition I would probably be totally into it.

A question I often ask myself: why aren't there any squirrels in our park like in New York's Central Park? So I type "squirrel" + "city" into Google. But the search machine is no help. Is it because of the types of trees? You would think they'd like beech trees, beechnuts, hazelnut shrubs, hazelnuts. I know so little.

And then I wonder where all the little critters are supposed to hide, like field mice and shrews, lots of birds live and breed in bushes too, and then the insects, spiders, butterflies, beetles, grasshoppers, and God only knows what else that has to rely on shrubs and hedges after practically everything that half-way resembles a weed has been dug up. Even bats sometimes live in bushes and they were quite a colony at certain times, dozens fluttering back and forth at nightfall on warm summer evenings, hectic zigzagging overhead, close to the water. It was beautiful.

And what about the foxes that raise their young here in the underbrush? I saw them crossing the street at night in the snow and often heard them barking, a strange sound. Sometimes I would bring them a bowl of food. It was empty the following morning. Don't any of these park planners ever think of the extraordinary wildlife that has found a habitat practically in the middle of the city?

Wiped out.

Five days after the police raided the park, they're back again, the black refugees, in the same old place at the last remaining island of rhododendron where three paths come together. Surprise, surprise. With a lookout at every bend in the path. Even from afar you can hear the murmur of their deep, soft voices that sound so different from white men.

22 March

You can tell how long it's been since I've gone down to my archive and basement studio. The filmmaker has asked me for a description of a photograph taken by Benjamin Katz. Apparently he was impressed with what I told him about it. It's hanging on the wall down there.

It shows two artists, Georg Baselitz and Markus Lüpertz, in Amsterdam, 1989. It must be in a museum, white walls in the background, the two men striding past each other, as if heading for some distant, extremely important destination, both exactly alike, the typical masculine pose, hands in their pockets, open coats billowing behind them. They're identically dressed, too, all in black, both with the same incredibly possessive stride, and although you can only see Baselitz's face, you know perfectly well that Lüpertz must have exactly the same grave, manly expression—both of them acutely aware of their great gravity and dignity.

The photograph made such an impression on me, a disturbing one too because a woman would never ever dare to assume a pose like that, no matter how famous she was. People would be scandalized.

But when I saw that photograph I thought, that's exactly how I want to take over museum spaces someday.

And long, long before that, there was an LSD trip with the Salamander, I hadn't started calling him that yet, it was just before we got together. I was wearing a wide, very long black coat and crossing a large plaza with exactly the same expansive stride, purposeful, the momentum and the wind making the coat billow behind me. I was filled with a feeling of courage and strength.

That was long before my first art event.

Today the memory of a shoot for a TV news program comes back to me that is a little bit like that image. It was in 1990 and I'm marching with great determination through the rooms of an art museum with large-format pictures of mine mounted on the walls. Except that I'm wearing Chanel shoes and an elegant dress.

The director of the museum, Roland Wäspe, who had the courage to invite me for an exhibition after a crisis that lasted many years, later became a kind of mentor. He was the youngest director of a museum far and wide and I was the very first woman to have a solo show there, right after Donald Judd.

"The little woman with big pictures," the news anchor said lovingly.

He has since retired from his profession, he thought he was too old.

A magazine has asked for a portrait—they recently published an interview—followed by the inevitable question: when is your next exhibition?

But I don't just want to deliver, I want to wait until the time comes, until I can say: here, take a look, this works, I can stand behind it, it's good.

And I want to live!

"My" Zurich gallerist has always showed my work, regularly, whenever I was ready, without a contract; that's not something to take for granted. Silvio Baviera. We have always remained faithful to one another.

And the above-mentioned magazine was the first to publish photographs of my controversial installation—years ago.

How long has the subject matter of identity been included in the repertoire of the art-specific press? Not very.

It seems to me that I'm often too early with the things that I get involved in.

Time to prepare the meeting with the publisher tomorrow. I haven't been through the draft of the book for a long time. On leafing through it, I realize that my priorities have changed, that the poses I now consider good and suitable are different from the ones I liked in the beginning. It often takes some distance to "see" a work again.

23 March

Shooting the film about me and my work is expected to take two or three years. Spontaneously, the following occurs to me: suppose I continue making daily notes the whole time and without holding back, could they be used as a kind of skeleton? You could extract passages about certain subjects and in this way, you'd have something honest and unembellished to go on, and you could surely find pictures to illustrate that. Maybe the film-maker would voice preferences, suggest themes that would naturally flow into these daily entries. I could imagine that something similar already occurred to him long ago. Maybe even shooting the whole thing as a kind of filmed diary?

That would take courage (on my part) and a whole lot of faith in the filmmaker. There are memories in these notes that I have never talked about—to anybody. The whole point would be no censorship, from outside or inside.

The style in which I'm writing tells me that at least I'm doing it for an imaginary reader.

Two things were discussed at the meeting with the publisher: first, the date of publication. The publisher wants to postpone it and couple it with an exhibition. I want to stick to the date. And second, the biography that is to be published one or two years later, and how to finance it. There are foundations, organizations, cultural grants, luckily that's not my job.

It's so wonderful to fall asleep over a book in the middle of the afternoon, a patch of sun on my face, the black cat and the tabby cat at my feet, their gaze fixed on my closed eyes because—who knows?—I might just wake up, get up, and feed them.

The window is ajar, the sound of summer in the background, somebody playing the guitar far away in the park, happy people down at the lake.

The library is not far from the publishers, gives me the chance to bring back a few books and borrow two new ones, one of which I've been looking forward to for a long time. Both me and my husband had a cold coming on but ignored it. We're paying for it now. Or rather: I'm enjoying ill health.

The moment, the present—if there was the least bit of magic in it—has always been more important to me than what the future would have to offer if I fulfilled all my obligations. Do I even have obligations? Is anybody waiting for me to do a new exhibition? Ambition?

I've done what I have to do. More than has so far been acknowledged.

If books were the only thing in the world, it would be worth living just for them.

After my mother died, I was astonished to find a large, thoughtfully equipped library. Including all the modern classics. They say that she was addicted to reading. And even though her life was a failure, she still had this one pleasure, at least when they hadn't "put her away" in a clinic because of her depression. She too was regularly removed by her autocratic husband whenever there was a problem. That's what clinics were for.

I have to stop myself. I'm slithering into something I don't want to deal with, not now, I was so happy a minute ago.

It's all right now, it's over.

24 March
As a child I sensed that something was not quite right in the relationship between the sexes. I couldn't put my finger on it because

the circumstances were veiled and I think, if you take a really close look, they still are. It's just different today.

The women's movement was still a long way away. Let's not forget that it was not until February 1971 that women in Switzerland were granted the right to vote!

One thing I did know at a very early age: I was not going to live the life of the women around me. Children and family were out of the question. I couldn't understand how anybody would aspire to being dependent on a man, and one single one at that, a whole lifelong, which is what happened to my mother with four daughters. (She had such a hard time.) Besides, men seemed to have a freedom that women didn't have and couldn't get. I couldn't fathom why men were so domineering or how they could find women desirable and even indispensable yet still be so disrespectful.

I wanted respect.

I have vivid memories of instinctively playing dumb as a young girl, and acting more helpless, too, when I had conversations with men because I knew perfectly well how that would please them. My girlfriends did exactly the same thing. We made them happy, it was easy to do, and they thought we were charming.

There is obviously no objective reason for women to act more helpless and less intelligent and talented than men but some girls still do that today. It's incredible, and it still works! So much has changed, and so little. Men still stick together in business, in politics, and at universities, and they are still reluctant about sharing their sinecures with women, which would have to be revamped anyway for women to be really happy in those positions.
And then, what about the children? Rare is the woman privileged enough to have a man in the background who will give her breathing space by taking over education and domestic duties—or at least half of them.

We've got a long wait ahead of us.

In how many movies did the especially desirous women play the dumbbell in those days? Think of the most famous sex symbol of all times, Marilyn Monroe. A "body" didn't have to be bright, in fact, it was a detriment. Marilyn's trick was to combine the body of a mature woman with the face and features of a very little girl, a sweet, helpless creature.

The recipe worked and I think men thought it was genuine.

The actress suffered because she probably realized she would never, never really be able to be just herself. She was spared the business of aging; it wouldn't have gone well. I did not look up to her.

In contrast to Marlene Dietrich. She was also extremely erotic, she was also adored, but I don't think men saw her as a seducible object. She attempted to walk the fine line between being a desirable woman and keeping control of the reins.

Everything about her was artificial, faked, there's no doubt about it. But with unbelievable authority, unbelievable artistry!

In an early interview I once called her the greatest living work of art.

Later she distanced herself from her film roles; she thought they were silly.

I think that's a pity.

I remember an interview with a journalist, extremely well in fact, who asked me about my first art event; it had caused quite a stir. I could tell right away that he wasn't taking me seriously. I was just an attractive, wacky girl producing stuff that he didn't understand. At some point, somebody who had accompanied him said that my father was the highly esteemed university professor that he, the journalist, had studied with. A change instantly came over his face: he became respectful, asked entirely different questions, and finally engaged in a serious conversation.

I guess he didn't realize that university professors can have dumb daughters, too.

Every woman knows what it's like; every woman could give accounts of such affronts.

Some get so used to it, they don't even notice it anymore.

Personally I've been less vulnerable to situations like that, but not so in my life as an artist because I have always worked with my own body, my woman's body. I don't have another one. I have always been aware of the ambivalence of this form of expression.

Men did the same things in those days but they were treated differently. You see it more clearly in retrospect.

"Do women have to be naked to get into the Met. Museum?" This question was posed by the Gorilla Girls, a feminist collective of women artists, who wish to remain anonymous. They've been organizing performances all over the world since 1985.

Because: "Less than 5% of the artists in the Modern Art Sections are women, but 85% of the nudes are female." Or: "Advantages of being a woman artist: having the opportunity to choose between career and motherhood" and "knowing your career might pick up after you're eighty."

They compiled a whole list on the subject.

We still live in a world that is designed primarily by men for men.

A reply has come in from the TV editor I had asked to do a show about "Fattenberg's verbal bloopers." She agreed that the issue was equally important and would address it, if at all possible.

The editor of a magazine emailed me that she has contacted a museum and has been assured that *The Salmon-Colored Boudoir* will be reconstructed next year. She is going to write about it. That's good, too.

And at night in the park, armed once again with scissors, string and suet balls, I run into another massive police raid with headlamps and search dogs tracking down drugs hidden, left behind in the rhododendron. It looks so ghostly, like a thriller, I hope they didn't think my suet balls were camouflaged drugs.

This morning: several suet balls are gone. Are they in a police laboratory? Morning coffee in the park restaurant, we talk about our dogs and cats, then about chickens, geese, and pigs which are supposedly particularly intelligent, oh, and a bear that scared my table companion once in Canada. She must be my age, beautifully done up, women can be beautiful in this age category, too, I must admit. If I were a man...

Are You Somebody? That's the title of the book I'm just reading by an interesting Irish writer around 50 years old. Her name is Nula O'Faolain.
I sure am.

They told her I was a well-known artist. A nice stranger wants to know if I'm still doing art.
Well... not too much, at the moment. Life has priority. It's almost spring.

I think I would miss these casual encounters if I moved to the country, a thought I periodically entertain.

26 March
It's time to store my winter wardrobe in the cellar and bring up the lighter clothing.

Clothing and jewelry—a philosophy: I always created my own fashions and was not infrequently copied.

Chinese work clothes, that's my inspiration now: simple, severe, beautiful. I looked for a unisex design in the Chinese neighborhoods of Paris and New York and I found one that fit perfectly. I had a pattern made from it that's laid out and ready in my sewing room; having it tailored for me is a telephone call away. My specifications are simple: functional and aesthetic. I have to think of the Bauhaus philosophy. A purist pattern, because I still want to look stylish in ten years. And it has to suit every occasion, at work as well as in the evening with a turquoise velvet turban.

High heels make you look sexy but only if you're absolutely sure you won't have to jump onto a bus.

At home, a black kimono with its simple cut. I am sure that will suit me equally well later as an old, gray-haired woman.

But to be really honest: if the filmmaker saw me at home in the evening the way my husband sees me, no makeup, night cream on my face, the kimono possibly full of animal hair, I suspect it wouldn't be quite the way he envisions the protagonist of his upcoming movie.

There's another article of clothing that I really like: those long gowns, with a simple cut, the ones Arab men wear in the heat. I have a couple of them. There's a photograph of Erté wearing one in his garden in Tunisia, with a big straw sun hat, 95 years old, I love that picture. He designed costumes for the big erotic shows in Paris and for a lot of Hollywood movies.

(Incidentally, the picture was taken when he was about to remodel his house... What an optimist!)

My earliest fashion idols were not women but rather two male actors: Pierre Clémenti in his leather coat that had such a distinctive cut, walking stick with a silver knob, and a gold tooth—for instance, in Buñuel's *Belle de jour*. The other one was Humphrey Bogart—not his partner Ingrid Bergman—in an early film classic, *Casablanca*, unforgettable in his trench coat and fedora. For the longest time, the latter was practically my uniform.

I'm afraid the filmmaker won't find that particularly interesting and the following even less.

Namely jewelry: practically everything I own is of my own design because I am friends with a goldsmith.

But actually it was my husband who started having the titles of my exhibitions engraved on very wide, heavy silver bracelets, almost like handcuffs, and I've kept it up. (This all started with a specific telephone number engraved on a bracelet, namely his.)

By now, I have so many bracelets with different engravings that I could cover myself with them from wrist to shoulder.

In addition, a goodly number of hinged bracelets in silver or gold, each one of which has something to do with my life: a wedding band dangling from one, from long ago when there was only enough money to buy a gold-plated ring, the engraving now practically illegible, but December in any case. A gold nugget, a present from the goldsmith. A cross that belonged to my mother and has never been worn. A tiny silver egg that can be opened, with a lovely little erotic message once placed inside. A wee replica of a Chihuahua (my first dog) and a coral with a matching piece that the beautiful artist wore around his neck. A small gold watch in the shape of a sphere, with the miniature movement visible through the glass: the gift of a woman artist who loved me a very long time ago. A baby tooth, in a gold setting, entrusted to me by the deceased Baron von Beck. An ivory-colored domino, on the back of it the year 2004—what was the connection? I can't think of it. Finally, two amulets that are related to the origins of my current husband.

The date 23.1.84 is engraved on a heavy chain bracelet, a particularly important day, a good twenty years ago: the first day of my withdrawal. Another is ornamented with ivory-colored dice and still another with gold-plated dog tags, round and hexagonal ones, they come from animals whose ashes I keep in black porcelain containers. There's an extremely thin gold bangle that my mother wore, kept after she died, in spite of everything.

Sometimes I wonder whether someone else will own or even wear such extremely personal items someday.

Then there are ebony, ivory, horn, and tortoise-shell armbands that have made a roundabout way into my collection, and honey or amber colored Bakelite bands, the predecessor of plastic introduced after the turn of the 19th century and yielding these distinctive colors. And ones out of mother-of-pearl. And jagged, coarse bracelets of heavy iron. Will they all end up in a dump someday?

27 March
Meeting in the morning about a workshop plus lecture planned for the fall in connection with an exhibition. Where, much to my great delight, I will see my beloved friend with a double name again, she will give a lecture as well. Her subject: politics. Mine: identity.

With a pang of concern I wonder what will happen someday with my collection of beloved objects, the ones that have accumulated throughout a lifetime in my mirror room and my work room.

Almost all of them have cropped up in one way or another in one or another of my works;

hardly surprising, I would be hard put to separate life and work.

Shells of all kinds in every conceivable color and shape, huge and small, some almost suggestive in shape. Iridescent white to tender pink, from cream to salmon colored, dotted or striped, too. Some dull outside and shiny inside. Tapered to a point and others with zigzag edges. Shaped like a bowl, the inside all mother-of-pearl. Some with chaste openings and others almost obscene.

Some particularly suggestive shells are ensconced in my very first installation, "served up" on a small, sumptuously decorated, semicircular table to the left of my satin bed.

For my exhibition in Genoa, I had a number of identical, salmon-red shells mounted on pedestals and variously labelled, with lights inside them, used to illuminate a large room, covered with black fleece. It looked very mysterious.

The photographer Alberto Terrile, took a picture of one for me, for a postcard, the model for it still sits far to the left on my dressing table and the plaque reads "Arte."

Then there are other wondrous underwater objects in my home like starfish, the sweeping shells of large aquatic snails, and sponge-like or translucent, filigree items that are hard to describe.

A whole universe.

Crystal balls and glass spheres. Bought a particularly large crystal ball from a gypsy in Vienna after an exhibition that had not made me particularly happy. Another given to me by a fortune-telling friend of mine, completely undeserved, and other balls that have made their way into my home here and there.

Superstitious I am not.

Perfume, a diverse collection, the volume of which doubled after a tragic death. There are bottles and flacons, shapes both whimsical and severe, round or angular, tall and slender, small and wide, shaped like a closed lotus blossom, another in the shape of a woman's body. With gold or silver colored lids, with crystal or cut glass stoppers. Others with a cupola, star, a coral, or two lovebirds on top.

A unique one, almost empty, of thick fluted glass with a gold colored screw off lid—you can still smell the scent—I've been saving it for years. It comes from the artist Sonja Sekula, because she's the one who took me in, took me to her house from the psychiatric clinic where we had met when I was still a very young girl, and that's how I came to this city. In the meantime—after having long been successful in the USA—she has finally become well known here, too.

If only she had suspected.

This happened long after her suicide.

These glass objects are in my "cabinet of curiosities." The bottom mundanely filled with my catalogues and books but the top containing framed photographs of people from my life. One picture is especially dear to me, of my husband and me, lovingly facing one another, with a cat that he had brought along from Amsterdam, early one morning when I was still in bed.

There's also a portrait of the artist El Lissitzky and one of Giuseppe Penone with reflecting lens on his pupils. And there's a picture of James Lee Byars' gold-plated bronze phallus as well as a reclining Brâncuși head, also gold colored. And so on.

But behind those things, well hidden, several porcelain jars and some of silver colored metal containing the ashes of my deceased animals.

But only I know that.

Then there are the large so-called factice bottles, most of them a gift from my young husband. But the most beautiful perfume bottle of all is still the one for Chanel N° 5, unsurpassed in the stringency of its shape.

In *Manon's Ambulance Service*, this cream-colored, streamlined ambulance, I have Chanel N° 5 trickling out of the IV.

On the other hand, in my installation *Das Damenzimmer*, also in the possession of a museum, I dedicated a satin-lined chest to fashion designer Coco Chanel—in black, that seemed fitting to me.

Eggs. Ostrich and rhea eggs, white, black, and ivory with a hand-caressing surface. Smaller birds' eggs, too, gray and speckled in black-and-white. Even artificial eggs, out of glass, in linden green and in blue, of ivory and of Bakelite, with tiny hinges and an ivory bowl inside. My first husband recently brought it back from a trip to India; it is the bowl of eternal youth, I won't say no to that. There's also a gold colored one, its contents remain a secret. The most unusual egg is only five centimeters tall but rather heavy, burgundy red and studded with an intricate pattern of rhinestones. It stands on silver feet and has a hinge, that means it can be opened and in the black interior lies a black pearl. An early mini copy of a Fabergé egg, to be precise. One day it was standing there in the midst of lipstick and compacts, I almost overlooked it: my husband had unearthed it in Vienna.

That reminds me of my very first art object, long before I had made a name for myself; it also had to do with eggs. It was an oval bowl of metal, with a good dozen plaster eggs piled up inside. The hand of a mannequin led to a round clock face in black-and-white, flanked by medical pliers. I can't remember if I was aware of the symbolism of the subject matter. In any case, the arrangement is reminiscent of those by Daniel Spoerri, who was already up and coming at the time. The work was shown, I even remember the name of the gallery; it's not listed anywhere. But there's a very small photograph of it, one of those with a white zigzag border. I probably left the object behind during one of my many moves.

In the meantime, I've started working with eggs again, mostly ostrich eggs, both broken and intact. The installations are pictured here and there.

Unforgettable, by the way, are the oversized eggs of white polyester that Herbert Distel, an artist from Bern, set adrift on the river Aare. He even sent one off to cross the Atlantic. He was still very young. I was enthralled. What I would have given to be able to buy one of his objects. Later I thought of offering to give him one of my works in exchange but I didn't think I was famous enough. One of his eggs would still be on my wish list today. But he went to live abroad long ago.

One egg that I have exists only as a photograph. It's a slightly elongated, particularly magical egg of white marble, *Sculpture for the Blind (Beginning of the World)*. Brâncuși made it in 1916. The photo is currently with some of the real eggs described above, lying on a pretty little black Bauhaus-period table, to which I applied an ivory colored chessboard pattern.

Skeletons of tiny little birds' heads, beak and spine included.
    The skull of a larger animal I can't identify with six teeth on each side, recently given to me by a former student of acting, now a TV actor. (For months I was addicted to a weekly show that he was in.)
    And then the head of a dead fox that I found in the forest, took it home and taxidermied it myself. Put it out on the balcony to dry, and

next thing: glorious, big, green, shiny beetles, had never seen the likes of them before, appear out of nowhere to suck up the tiniest remains.

A delicate primate skull, from the Salamander I think, has found a permanent home on a black table to the right of the bed, in the midst of all the other special things in the *boudoir.*

Almost forgot to mention a human skull with a circular hole right next to the temple, a projectile. The statute of limitations has probably expired for the crime, I mean my crime: namely, stealing it from the catacombs in Paris. The skull has made several appearances in my work, for example, as a photograph in the series *Forever Young*, for galleries in Milan and Chicago, afterwards on view at "my" Zurich gallery. On the back of a catalogue, I embellished it with a phallic, pink cardboard nose.

Birds' Nests simply can't be ignored. They have to be taken along. Some are soft and upholstered, some tattered, others a perfect, dense weave, and in all sizes. Found over the years, for the most part after a storm. Curiously serendipitous contents: chewing gum wrappers, even coins, feathers obviously, human hair, bits of string, and this and that.

Fans in white and black and red, tender pink as well, matt and lacquered. Big ones and small ones, round, oval, solid, and others that can be opened. Huge fans made of feathers, some out of linen, and also of painted paper.

Like many of the things named above, there are several in my twelve-cornered cabinet, made of fluffy rose colored or white feathers, and one out of a palm leaf.

At least two play a role in the above-mentioned photographic project, *Forever Young*, one in the shape of an inverted heart is even pictured on the cover of the catalogue.

And so everything ends up in my work, sooner or later.

Or is it the other way around?

But the feathers!

Swan feathers. Ostrich feathers. Guinea fowl feathers. Feathers from Reeves pheasants. From ducks and peacocks. Jaybird feathers. Marabou feathers. Feathers from ravens. Pigeon feathers.

Feathers from gold pheasants and from silver pheasants. Even some eagle feathers.

Some have been dyed, like the ones used for costumes in Parisian vaudeville. Or long slender, pointed feathers, speckled black on brown. Others in delicate pastels with rounded ends. Some curved and arched, in linden green with black tips. Or white ones with a dark quill, and rounded feathers with a mother-of-pearl sheen.

They used to be beautifully tailored embellishments on women's hats, one of the last remaining milliners in our city had to file for bankruptcy and sold me a goodly number or, to be more precise, practically gave them to me.

I could continue describing some more of these particularly pretty, though not uncommonly costly items.

50 things to do before you die: That was the name of a BBC TV program. One of them: to part with things.
I can't. I can't do it. Not yet.

28 March
But what to do with the files overflowing with negatives, probably more than thirty, stashed away in what was once a broom closet? Never looked at them again.

Managed to persuade my husband today to ransom another dog from the animal shelter in Paris; the suffering there is great. At the same time I tell him about my passionate wish to spend another half year in a studio at the Cité internationale des arts in the same city, actually, a very specific studio: the one with windows facing the Seine. Because in the evening when the tourist boats glide by with all their little lamps, the lights pass slowly and silently across the ceiling of the entire room. Magic.

But animals are not allowed there.

Those two wishes are equally intense.

The filmmaker is thinking of shooting in Paris, and of the trip there.

My vision of the trip: a closed compartment in the train, which I've converted into an extravagant, elegant little chamber, fitted out for a prolonged trip. In my mind's eye I see pictures of the Sternberg classic with Marlene Dietrich and her companion, a mysterious Asian woman that I liked almost more than the main character: the movie was called *Shanghai Express.*

The documentary filmmaker probably wouldn't come up with an idea like this.

I hear the monotonous clatter of the carriage wheels, feel the jiggling, the landscape outside, gray in gray, nothing else. Then one could fade into the black-and-white shots that we took back then in the train from Paris to Zurich; they are enlarged on mat board, a little bit grainy, my head still shaved bare. But in a second or possibly third class compartment.

I have memories of a compartment in the train from Zurich to Genoa, my current husband and me, two dogs, three cats, and considerable luggage. We had reserved the whole compartment. A kitty litter under the seat, the cat beds on the hat racks. A place found for the water and feeding bowls. We settled in, domestic bliss, with the lovely picnic that we had taken along. It was an unforgettable half-year trip to a studio in Italy where we stayed for half a year.

Have just seen Peter Liechti's film *Hans im Glück* (Lucky Jack) on TV—for the third time—such a wonderful, wonderful filmmaker. Again, had I not known better, I would have started zapping around within the first 10 minutes. But then suddenly you get sucked in, you can't, don't want to look away even though the subject matter has absolutely nothing to do with you or your interests, and the images don't either. On the surface, it's about nothing more earth-shattering than a man who wants to stop smoking. In actuality, it's about everything, about the great, overarching whole, about life and death, and it's a wonderful film and the filmmaker, by the way, a wonderful person.

Equally unforgettable, the film he made with the artist and explosives expert Roman Signer from eastern Switzerland. I once even curated *Signer's Suitcase* at a cultural center. Later the filmmaker told me that the collaboration ultimately cost them their friendship.

Be that as it may: I want "my" film to be about "everything," too.

Earlier on in my notebooks I came across comments on how I would envision this film if the circumstances were different, and the filmmaker too. Perhaps I should read through them again.

At any rate, you could already tell there was fierce opposition on my part.

29 March

Also just found and read some biographical notes in the computer, notes that I made for the journalist but never dared to show her because I was too embarrassed. They describe the time prior to the years in Paris. Should the filmmaker read them?

Finally saw the Chinese film *2046* directed by Wong Kar-Wei. It's very long and, at times, I couldn't quite follow the plot, but the work of cameraman Christopher Doyle blew my mind, kept taking my breath away—literally! Stylized images, sensual, bewitching, enigmatic, bittersweet, glamorous, hypnotic, melancholy, hopelessly romantic, stunningly beautiful. The soundtrack with opera arias and songs by Nat King Cole and classical symphonies and mysterious background noises equally enthralling.

A melodrama of perfection.

I dream about images like that.

30 March

A similar approach could be used for the Hôtel Saint-Jacques in Paris—in case they decide to do some shooting in the place where I took my first photos for *la dame au crane rasé* (the woman with shaved head). The room an entirely self-contained world: the small space with rose-patterned wallpaper, flowered bedspreads, our gas camping cooker, our trunk painted salmon pink, scattered clothing, the working table on top of the bed due to lack of space, the broken window pane, the bidet and the sink with picture postcards all around the mirror, and strips of negatives hung up on a string. There was even one of those typical French fireplaces, the ones that usually come with a mirror, but sealed off ages ago.

A photo series bears witness to that time.

And then the steep, narrow stairs and narrow corridors, all the doors numbered.

And the acoustic memories, I loved listening to the sounds of life all around.

We improvised some of the photographs in the laundry room, that contained the only bathtub in the building, a hip bath, not particularly clean incidentally, filled with water from a black rubber hose.

For a while my partner and I rented a tiny room opposite as well, I think it was number 13, and converted it into a dark room.

The hotel still exists, I know it, but it's most likely been renovated. At the time it was an extremely inexpensive student hotel that offered monthly deals.

Just as filmable, the flat of my Parisian friend Susi, known as "Suzy" in the French press, on Avenue René Coty. It was also the setting for a number of shots in the above-mentioned series. (The owner was on vacation, with Salvador Dalí in Cadaqués, no less.) For example, on the roof of the building is an angel with great wings that has just landed on the chimney.

The private roof terrace was the site of the well-known portraits against the backdrop of the city.

A huge corner sofa in dark velvet, in front of heavy gold-framed mirrors, became the backdrop for rather outré glamour shots. I was wearing Susi's long-haired black coat on the secret stairs—a spiral staircase. She told me later it was monkey fur.

The *appartement* has since deteriorated; the wallpaper—still the same color, a dark purple, I think—all tattered and coming off the walls.

Nonetheless, there are no lodgings like Susi's in all of Paris.

As far as I know, it was a gift of Paul Getty, the elderly American-British multimillionaire, who has since died. Or at least he gave her a down payment for it—it was new and luxurious then—along with a monthly appanage. Because Susi was not only pretty and sexy, but also amusing and witty.

In any case she took regular trips to Mr. Getty in London and was acquainted with quite a number of "important" or famous people.

Another possibility would be the building where my then partner and I lived the longest in Paris,

4 rue du Liban. Parisian television had hired him as a "girl Friday." Scheduled for demolition, but it's still there! Here, too, the "kitchen" consisted of a small gas camping cooker, we often had Merguez sausages and home-made chips. What furniture we had—a giant mattress on the floor with lots of pillows, a door on trestles as a table, and even a pretty decent sofa, reminiscent of the Bauhaus, in the room next door, that could also be used as a bed—were pieces we found on the street because when people move in Paris they often leave what they don't need out in front of the building. Very important and our pride and joy was a wardrobe from a junk store in Paris, elegantly curved and beautifully lacquered with cut-glass mirrors on the doors.

A small section of wall, painted gray, with a naked bulb dangling from the cable, provides the background for two extravagant series of photographs, much published and exhibited later on.

A Swiss journalist came to Paris and wrote a pretty detailed article. In the photograph I'm standing—very glamorous, by the way, and on the cover of the magazine—in front of this partially boarded-up building.

Not to forget a modest weekend house in Geneva where my partner and I squatted for a couple of weeks after we came back to Switzerland. The owner had died and we found out that the place was abandoned. It's hardly worth describing the furniture out of particle board and plywood. At least there was a low couch that was the exact length of the tiny room.

There we produced a 33-part series of photos, still in black-and-white, that prefigured the theme of the new series *Einst war sie Miss Rimini.* I called it the *Ball der Einsamkeiten* (Dance of Solitudes).

After that, we parted ways.

Galleries in Switzerland, Germany, and France soon had shows of the above-mentioned photos, followed by museums in Amsterdam and Düsseldorf. After an exhibition at Kunsthaus Zürich, the above-named series became the very first photographic work to be bought for the collection of the museum—thanks to director Erika Billeter—along with the cycle *dame au crane rasé.*

Up till then, photography had always been written off as "applied art."

They told me the exhibition drew record numbers of visitors. In any case, the museum's magazine had several double-page spreads with several pictures of the show and the Swiss Arts Council Pro Helvetia financed a catalogue. Unfortunately, the catalogue, as well as the first and second book, are now out of print.

Oh, and by the way, David Bowie bought one of my pictures in Geneva...

31 March
Yesterday, lost or left my black leather bag somewhere, my favorite at the moment, luckily neither keys nor diary in it, but money, maybe 200 francs, no idea, ID card, blood group card, vaccination certificate, doctor's certificate for agoraphobia and claustrophobia (in case I get into a precarious situation), credit cards (instantly blocked them), library card, museum cards, train card, business cards, bus card, digital camera with pictures and extra battery, notebooks, ballpoint pens, compact, vanilla-colored cloth bag with all kinds of makeup accessories, too much trouble to list them all, broken horn comb, silver pill box with contents for emergencies, including one Valium 10, aspirin, one Xenical,

one Ponstan, and small plastic containers with dog cookies...

Financial loss only the camera and compact, but what a hassle. It would've been easy for the finder to call me. Everything besides the money and the camera will probably end up in the lake.

Just ran into Pipilotti at the entrance to the park, with husband and child, a little boy with dark hair and a pageboy haircut, who looks like me she thought. She had just come back from Brazil and said that Pierre M. told her about "my" film and that he's been asked to work on it and that he is a fabulous cameraman that she loves to work with and who, incidentally, knows Wong Kar-Wai and his films inside out!

I'm happy! What more could I want? I'm seeing the filmmaker tomorrow. It's all good.

1 April
The filmmaker is beginning to "see" and to feel the film and I like what he tells me about it. He really senses how I have spent my life isolating myself, no matter where I was. Everywhere I created these "artificial paradises," as he calls them, from which I would look out at the world.

I like the idea of starting with that thought. Because my first installation was exactly that: a thoroughly artificial paradise. Before that, the Salamander and I had created a refuge for ourselves for a couple of years between screen dividers in a gigantic attic at the very top of a building in the old town, and the entrance was a kind of wardrobe that you had to walk through. If you weren't in the know, you would never have guessed that people were living behind it. We had no warm running water and no kitchen, only a single hotplate on an old chest of drawers, and I used to go to a hippie commune to wash our linens, and the toilet was on the ground floor but we were living on the fourth floor. Not only that, the WC had two toilets and we shared them with a "club for lonely gentlemen," the name of a strange association that had parties twice a week on the floors below— and unknowingly paid for the electricity bill for our floor as well.

In spite of all that, these funky accommodations turned into an almost elegant island and acted more than once as a backdrop for photo series in fashion magazines. Hard to believe, but it's true.

The telephone rings, a man's voice speaking broken German, he found my wallet, no money but all of the bank cards. He can hand it over to me at the station. He arrives half an hour late, a nice Portuguese man. I give him 50 francs, then, looking through it, I discover an African telephone card... Something's fishy. But what?

2 April
The police seemed to be targeting the African dealers again. One of their cars is parked in the same spot practically all day. Does it make a difference? In any case, at night the regulars were back as usual.

They have nothing to lose!
It's an illusion to think that police raids can resolve the refugee issue.

Am working on my "year in snapshots." They would make a good book as well, a very thick photo book. Maybe people would be interested in them after my biography is published. I'm beginning to see how I might design it.
And I'm also getting a vague idea of how some of them could come together as an exhibition.
Like I said before: I'd give anything for a big white room, completely empty except for a computer. There are hundreds of photographs

to look at, thousands in fact, to be arranged and put in context and to decide on a sequence that is dynamic and exciting. I have to find a solution. It's impossible here.

We each sit in our respective studies, my husband and I, doors open. At tables covered with paper, tons of paper, the piles keep growing, now covering parts of the floor and the furniture and the windowsills. He's preparing lectures, I rummage through photographs. He's listening to loud music, the "new" Lou Reed; I'm listening to loud music, the "new" Paolo Conte. They merge in the hall, it sounds seriously beautiful.

Lou Reed used to mean a great deal to me. When my third husband was still a teenager and before we had met, *Walk on the Wild Side* was the title I gave to a large-scale installation-cum-performance at Kunsthaus Zürich with about 60 extras: thirty men and thirty women. That was shortly before I went to Paris. And *Kicks* from Coney Island Baby was the song I chose for my show of seven men as art objects in the windows of the Jamileh Weber Gallery in Zurich. The Salamander played a kind of rock star for me; he was the centerpiece of the "picture." The performance—I called it *Manon Presents Man*—was inspired by the windows in which hookers ply their wares in Hamburg or in Amsterdam. Except that the live people on display were men.

Paolo Conte became a fixture in my life during the half year I spent in Genoa. That was much later. I was preparing an exhibition at the Palazzo Ducale and was sick the whole time, but I love him.

3 April

My beautiful table companion with the big dog, a briard with short curly hair and red, of course, just like hers, told me quite a bit about her life over coffee yesterday. If you've led a committed, courageous life, you have something to say as of a certain age.

If I had to describe how my days begin, it would be pretty much the same, namely, dictated by the animals:

First thing, coat thrown over pajamas, a short, invariably urgent walk around the building. Every day I hope I won't run into anybody on the stairs, because I don't yet look very much like the person people know from photographs. Then the feeding of the cats and dogs, the cats are already waiting in line. Then clean the litter box. Next, see to the oldest cat because she's not in good health any more. I do that well, I'm the best animal nurse far and wide. I can administer medication, insert a drip, give injections, and the animals don't mind. Besides, nothing can disgust me, the same goes for people, by the way.

And then in the winter the birds on the terrace also want to be fed.

I gave my favorite cat the lethal injection myself—after getting exact instructions. I didn't want a stranger to do it. She knew exactly that I wanted only the best for her. She had advanced cancer, I first gave her painkillers so that we would have a day together to say goodbye. I will never forget those intensely intimate hours, we looked each other in the eyes the whole time.

I've always been able to envision an entirely different life, or better yet, a second, parallel life, life in a simple, remote house with a garden, the house full of animals. (The filmmaker will squirm when he reads this because he doesn't share my interests.)

There was a time when my career as an artist was pretty iffy and I was about to train in another field. Maybe I could've been happy that way, too, maybe much happier, who knows.

Plants are next, my second love, they're also living creatures and therefore given privileged treatment.

There is this beech tree that wanted to live with me and has taken up residence in the southwest corner of the terrace. It needs a bigger pot every year and a lot of water every day and I like being responsible for its well-being. And then in spring, usually mid-May, two smaller trees are delivered that have spent the winter in a greenhouse. They're called cabbage trees and to me as a lay person they look like filigree palm trees. I'd like to have a special cactus plant (I don't know the name of it) this year on a lovely little round cast-iron table, its lilac-colored stone top cracked this winter because the sun is relentless here at the lake.

The herbs are on the side of the terrace: basil, rosemary, peppermint (these three fragrances!), parsley, and so on. Sometimes I plant tomatoes, tie them up on the window bars, and when I touch their leaves, my hand smells curiously wonderful for a long time. I'm an amateur, don't have a green thumb, pretty ignorant, but I can't do without plants. To have a garden, just once in my life...

Two or three friends share my joys. The Salamander thinks there should be a book someday about "Manon and Animals," probably echoing Colette and her animals. She was clearly a city person and yet still deeply loved plants and animals; they made her happy and in that respect she is a model for me.

"Regarde," she supposedly said shortly before she died, pointing to a flower in a vase next to her bed.

I don't doubt for a single second that that really happened.

Now it's the kitchen's turn. My husband is a wonderful cook but the kitchen is a total wreck afterwards, which Alice Schwarzer might suspect and not entirely without justification.

Caution: I love Alice Schwarzer, she was such a courageous feminist and they gave her so much grief. Where would we be without her? It would probably take several books to describe what we have to thank her for—both men and women. My husband and I heard a lecture of hers in Zurich. She was so charismatic, captivated the audience with great humor and charm, and her rhetorical skills were impressive.

I would have liked to thank her personally for the long article she wrote about my work that was even honored with a picture on the cover of *Emma*. (Which disturbed quite a few readers and provoked indignant letters to the editor because of my naked bosom.) The words under the cover photograph read: "MANON—why *Emma* bares her breasts six years after the *Stern* trial."

But I was much too shy to go up to Alice Schwarzer. I was afraid she might be disappointed because what she knew about me was only from photographs and the written interview.

That happens to me a lot.

Mostly with people I haven't known for a long time. I feel so reluctant, bashful, almost like a child. And that makes me back off.

Today's children don't have that problem, thank God.

Back to my morning: haven't mentioned the half hour of gymnastics that I do most of the time or, to be more precise, on-and-off, and then the dip in the lake until well into the cold time of year. (All of this can, of course, be nullified at any time by urgent organizational or other duties in the field of art. Then things get tight.)

Years ago when I was young, taking a winter walk in the Tiefenbrunnen baths, snow on the ground, I saw a group of older people, men and women in bathing suits, laughing and joking as they galloped across the meadow and dipped into the ice cold lake.

Someday I want to be an old person like that, too, I thought.

But everything was different then. I used to live at night. The shutters of the windows and the dark red velvet curtains stayed closed during the day; I didn't want to see the light. Instead of real flowers, I preferred ones out of mother-of-pearl and created my own extremely personal island around the big bed. I didn't get up until the afternoon, worked until midnight, and then went out. Alone, if possible, that was important to me. I went out towards midnight and that was exciting because night people are different.

"Isolation and loneliness" is what my multitalented artist friend writes to me, "the telephone doesn't ring anymore."

Recently there was a long article about him in the *New Yorker*, and his last big book of photographs is one of the most beautiful.

The telephone never meant a lot to me, often I just don't answer.

I don't want an answering machine either; the idea of having to call back a number of people in the evening doesn't appeal to me. If it's really important, I'll find out about it sooner or later. If I have to speak to someone, I feel incredibly shy about taking the receiver and actively invading someone's world. It's so intrusive.

When you are hopelessly in love, you do sit on the phone for hours and sometimes whole nights through, and my husband and I speak on the phone several times a day, but that's different.

Back to a second life that I could just as easily envision. There were times when nothing was happening in my profession, but I survived. That's because I didn't put all my eggs in one basket. My happiness never relied exclusively on my ambitions as an artist. Certainly there was sometimes a sense of regret, never having received the really great recognition to which, in my modest opinion, I would be entitled, even though the signs are slowly changing. There were always other sources of happiness.

I have to think of that every time a man has killed himself, sometimes taking his entire family along with him, because of professional troubles, because he didn't get a promotion or was fired or didn't get the recognition he expected. Standing on your own two or, even better, three legs is a great deal safer than standing on one.

4 April
The same presumably applies to the loss of youth and beauty: if a woman banks on looks alone, she'll have a hard time later. Although I must admit, the attention showered on attractive people can vastly enhance their quality of life, and it is tempting to take advantage of that.

While in Paris, I tried out both.

Sometimes I was out and about, a nondescript person with no makeup; other times all dressed up and conspicuous. "La vache ce qu'elle est belle," two male teenagers said in typical Parisian slang, impressed when I stepped out of the hotel on Rue St-Jacques, in fresh makeup for a posh appointment.

What I hadn't expected was that men approach inconspicuous women much more readily: they seem to be more accessible.

The magnolia is in bloom. I have been immeasurably happy all day long today, and actually for no reason at all.

5 April

The marathon passing by in front of our house,
like every year, from Enge to Meilen and back,
a total of 42 km. Long-legged Africans like
gazelles heading up the pack, seemingly ef-
fortlessly. Followed after a while by the locals,
driven by ambition, their faces distorted from
the strain. They say it should take about five
hours; the 20-year-old Kenyan winner, lightly
striding all the way, manages in 2 hours, 10
minutes, and 16 seconds. The fastest woman
takes 2 hours, 34 minutes, and 39 seconds.
30 people are injured, 15 need an infusion.

Today's program: prepare the CD for the *MISS
RIMINI* book; the photographs in the computer
all have a few identifying words and a number.

For example:

"Mother-in-law with bouquet
for hospital visit, very worried, no. 18"

"Still alone,
costume ball the morning after, no. 13"

"Nun, with glasses
and holding an apple, no. 57"

"Chemotherapy patient in hospital shirt,
from the back, drip, no. 43"

"Friendly Salvation Army woman, no. 6"

"Domina in action,
in black latex and masked, no. 71"

"Well-to-do blonde woman with large beige
hat and pearl necklace, no. 12"

"Hooker in Amsterdam, not quite sober,
negligée on the tasteless side, no. 97"

"Nursing home, woman with walker, slightly
deranged, no. 1"

"Beautiful blonde with long hair and black
hat, radiant, no. 18"

"Lesbian with tie and cigarette,
flirting, no. 82"

"Middle-aged woman in dowdy
pink underwear in a good mood, no. 20"

"Waitress, close to nervous breakdown,
open blouse, no. 31"

"Homeless person, desperate and
scarred by alcohol, no. 19"

"Self-confident woman in a Chanel dress with
jewelry and a little notebook, no. 97"

"Naked stripper with gold mask,
wanton, no. 59"

"Researcher in white protection clothing
and mask, two rats, no. 16"

"Woman in St. Moritz with mink coat
and little dog, no. 21"

"Widowed teacher, retired early, no. 45"

"Actress with wig cap before going on stage,
still playing the lover, no. 58"

"Patient in straitjacket,
panic and confusion, no. 2"

"Marlene Dietrich double performing
with accordion, no. 27"

"Mediterranean woman, just arrested,
with handcuffs, no. 101"

"Housewife waiting for daughter-in-law,
still in curlers, dangling cigarette, no. 7"

"Bride, no longer quite young,
on the arm of her groom, no. 12"

"Broadway actress with gold turban,
facing the photographer, no. 43"

And 24 more, there were over 50 portraits of women.

And then the objects for which there was no room in the exhibition, like "Telephone cable, no. 27" or "Bride's veil, no. 30" or "Pink powder puff, no. 10," and so on. Roughly 100 items were photographed, maybe about twelve will be reproduced in the book.

It's like that every time.

But that also makes me see things more clearly—I gradually get an overall picture—though the sequence might change at the last minute, if necessary, for a hopefully interesting result.

Maybe there's also room for some empty space?

6 April
The fishing boats came back long ago. At the lake children have built fragile towers out of stone. Another child is drawing an animal in chalk on the flagstones. Lovers can't stop touching each other; it's a lovely sight.

The MISS RIMINI photos, mounted on aluminum and already exhibited for the first time, are coming back today from a second show organized by the city of Zurich. The canton of Zurich purchased the entire series of about 50 works, paying, I was told, the highest price ever for a work of art.

The accompanying book is about to go to press.

7 April
The past is getting longer and the future shorter.

The show of video films is opening at Kunst-museum Bern tonight. Haven't seen my own film for a long time, the one made in Lucerne in 1979 for my photo exhibition, *dame au crane rasé.*

A good reason for me and my husband to meet the Salamander, who lives in the country's capital and has long been our best friend.

In the days of the legendary curator Harald Szeemann at the Kunsthalle, it was always worth taking a trip to Bern for us youngsters from Zurich. Urs Lüthi and I also regularly visited Toni Gerber's gallery there although I was still miles away from launching into performance. The scene in Bern was hopping: I'm thinking of Markus Raetz, Balthasar Burkhard, Jean-Frédéric Schnyder, Herbert Distel, Franz Gertsch, Esther Altdorfer, Meret Oppenheim. And I remember the German painter and collagist Michael Buthe, especially his glitter pictures and the little glitter books that we used to pass around. Not to mention Katharina Sieverding, a tall German woman my age, extremely self-confident and extremely sexy. She worked with photography and was married to somebody named Klaus. That was all we knew at the time. The disappointment in the men's faces was unmistakable when they found out. In any case, we used to meet at the same events and every single one of those artists has since risen to fame.

Mustn't forget Jean-Christophe Ammann either, who subsequently organized spectacular exhibitions at Kunsthaus Luzern at which we were also regulars. His exhibition "Transformer: Aspects of Travesty" was the zeitgeist in a nutshell. I knew some of the contributing artists and a few people in the audience were wearing extravagant, glittery jackets that I designed, it was pretty exciting.

A year later I had the opportunity to do a performance of my own there, *The End of Lola Montez*.

Speaking of a place to work, a wonderful possibility has come up: the Metropol building is empty at the moment and I might be able to rent a room of 100 square meters in it. The agent wants to contact the city of Zurich. I'm sure the mayor's office will recommend me. Wouldn't that be wonderful? A big, empty, white room!

8 April
Bern: my video was intentionally juxtaposed with the work of my ex-husband, that's not

new. Curators occasionally do that when they show my pictures because they know that we were once a couple. We are probably represented in the same collections.

I hadn't seen this video by my artist husband before, or had forgotten it. It's from the days when he was so incredibly beautiful, he really and truly was, anybody would fall in love with that video image.

What you see is his face to the left and to the right, a half-spilled glass of milk. Sporadically, the milk is poured over his face, you can't tell where it's coming from; his expression changes accordingly, he flinches just slightly, minimal mimicry, erotic, ravishing. The extraordinary purity of his facial features electrifies the work. This beautiful man was my husband.

My own video, made a few years later, may be erotic, but in an entirely different way, more aggressive, harsh and tender at once. Accompanied by a passage from Jean-Michel Jarre. Everyone knew his music at the time and it was a perfect fit. Actually the whole thing happened by chance. There was a video camera lying around when the first exhibition of my Parisian pictures closed in Lucerne, so we —the gallerist, my Parisian partner, and me—

thought we should take advantage of the opportunity. I had the idea of panning across the pictures very, very slowly, aiming the camera repeatedly at real heads in between, so you can hardly distinguish between photograph and real person— at most because of an eyelid or minimal movement of the mouth. This static approach appealed to me.

On the way back to Zurich I had an agonizing toothache. First an aspirin, then a couple of drops of Tramadol, then a Ponstan 500 plus a sleeping pill.

I think I'll make a list of things that I would need in the Metropol building.
What a beautiful way to work that would be, along the lake to Bellevueplatz, a quick cup of coffee there at the Odeon, walk across the bridge, a tiny stretch along the river, and then this incredibly beautiful building! It has to work.

Inquiry from Christa de Carouge, currently the most distinctive fashion designer in Zurich, whether I could do a performance of some kind at her fashion show. Her collections are extremely idiosyncratic: commodious, monk-like clothing, black for the most part, nothing extraneous, beautiful fabric, everything aesthetic and comfortable. Broadly speaking, like my own philosophy if that's what you want to call it. Although her designs are more suitable for bigger women.

Then there are other inquiries that I still have to check out.

Toothache still excruciating despite heavy-duty medication. Eclipses everything else. The leaves on the trees behind my bed seem to have grown a couple of centimeters; the red and white umbels have blossomed and I didn't even notice. Will undergo final treatment tomorrow so that I can participate in what's happening in nature and the world again.

Teeth: symbol of youth and health. I almost feel humiliated to think that something might be wrong with them because I want to keep them to the end. I already had to surrender a tooth, way back to the left. It's hard for me to admit that! But replacing it was no problem.

Took pictures yesterday in a photo booth at the railroad station, like teenagers, first my husband and me, then with the Salamander, and then all three of us together.

9 April
Dentist. At long last.

Meeting afterwards with the journalist who is writing the postscript for the *RIMINI* book.

She wants to replace the first photograph. I was dead set against it and finally realized she's right. Yes, she's right, and I'm glad she saw it.

For the cover, the designer suggests a playful font, probably perceived as feminine. In contrast, I want a bare-bones design. They accepted it. The final version will be sent to the publisher tomorrow.

10 April
Life has embraced me again, grateful and glad. The Pope is dead and Rome flooded with pilgrims. Harald Juhnke died. Charles is going to marry Camilla and the Prince of Monaco has also died. Stéphanie has a new husband and Caroline's husband is in hospital. So much for *Paris Match* and *die Bunte.* Spring rain, the greenery is growing so fast you can almost see it.

The meeting with the publisher went smoothly, not a single hitch. The publisher, the designer, and I now agree on everything; the book will come out at the end of May. It was originally planned for May 10. There will be an English version; I would like to have a French version too but the publisher is not oriented towards France. (My very first book was a great success in Paris.)

Pulsating toothache back again in the afternoon, so excruciating that I went straight to the dentist without an appointment, I didn't care, I wouldn't even have cared if they had pulled the tooth.

Life simply stops at moments like that, the world could come to an end if only the pain would go away. I have often heard older people complaining about tooth problems, I could never relate that to myself, thought I was invulnerable.

Filmmaker called, couldn't respond.

11 April
The filmmaker met the biographer. He told her he wanted the film's point of departure to be the present. But the course of my life is calm today, so diametrically opposed to what it used to be. I don't need spectacle anymore. My day-to-day life is rather uneventful nowadays (though eventful enough for me). What makes me happy now is contemplation, just looking

at everything, and not action. You can't film that. I don't know what I have to offer him.

Nowadays I am happy. In earlier days... well, I didn't really want to live, not that much anyway.

My anesthetic: pills and also work. You can't imagine two more divergent ways of life than that of the young woman of yesterday and the woman of today. Although the potential was already there: I had the capacity for happiness, there were flashes of the happiness I have now, but darkness dominated.

Now, with the distance of time, I've come to understand much of what oppressed me. The addiction to seduce, for example. The excitement when a man appealed to me. Would I succeed in seducing him, in "possessing" him, as men themselves would call it? I know now that it was a means of coping with depression because as long as the excitement lasted there was no room for anything else. It kept anxiety and depression at bay. All those countless affairs and falling in love over and over again: it was nothing but an attempt at self-therapy, nothing but a drug.

But at least I also benefited in a way because I learned so much about human nature. I am almost never mistaken about people and everything I'm capable of, everything I know I learned by watching men because my basic education is minimal. The carpenter showed me how to restore old furniture and even how to build a door, the gardener how to deal with plants, the veterinarian how to give an IV, the musician honed my ear, I argued with the intellectual, and the artist explained to me how the art world operates. (In the last case, I listened with only half an ear because, to this day, I don't get it, or rather, it doesn't interest me.)

In any case, there is not a single encounter that I regret. Not a single one.

In a way it was my second education.

Some of these people later turn up at my openings because lovers can become friends and I am unconditionally faithful as a friend.

Premier of *Katzenball*, a documentary about lesbian life in Switzerland. The filmmaker sent me tickets because she had interviewed me six years ago thinking that I might participate, but I felt I wasn't quite suited. The film is fabulous, and not only that, it's full of humor. It contains wonderful, perfectly assembled black-and-white shots from old news programs and advertising and early Swiss films. It just received a Teddy Award at the Berlinale, and well-deserved! The filmmaker told me that the prize was relatively unimportant, having been awarded in the category of queer films. Whatever. The oldest woman portrayed in the film is 92, a perfectly enchanting woman from French Switzerland. A prominent blonde fashion designer from Zurich also features in it; she looks fantastic. She already did in the days when we frequented the same clubs. She was a magnet who attracted people and I probably was, too. Later we both ran into hard times, but in different ways.

Tonight, at the very last second—I have a tiny reprieve over the weekend—I'm still amending the long finished book. Replacing portraits, changing the sequence, rearranging objects, rejecting everything, starting all over…

What am I after, what do I want to trigger in viewers?

I want them to be moved.

The costumes and objects used in the above photo project are gifts or loans or flea market discoveries.

For example, the pink garter: a rising star in the heaven of art—who later shone bright along with an artist friend in Berlin—sent it to me years ago, straight from Hollywood;

it comes from a silent film. The letter with it was written in red ink.

My husband recently came back from New York with a rapper's skull cap for me.

The elegant black mink coat plus mink hat belongs to my friend who lives in the same building as we do, which she did before too, when we had a different address; the same goes for the (imitation) ocelot coat.

Various satin tops are the sewn creations of my Parisian friend. I come across her once in a while in *Paris Match.*

The scarf is an item connected with my husband's whiplash.

My beautiful artist husband brought back a big gold flower brooch from a trip to Berlin, a long time ago.

Cycling helmet, jersey, and glasses are part of my first husband's current athletic gear.

The captain's hat belongs to a specific ship because I am in possession of a French captain's license for an 11-ton houseboat.

My GP gave me an IV stand plus drip to take along.

The leather jacket belongs to my husband along with the white dinner jacket plus red bow tie.

The little dog in one of the pictures, on the arm of a no longer that young but very beautiful and elegant blonde, was my Chihuahua named Missy (after writer Colette's girlfriend), who died of old age shortly after the picture was taken on a very hot day during the heatwave that summer.

I like the way in which the people and animals that figure in my life also infiltrate my work.

12 April
Melancholy can foster creativity, depression kills it.

Morning. Women's conversation. I love it: three entirely different women of about the same age, who have each lived rather long and entirely different lives. One of them, I just found out today, was a luxury call girl and has now become decidedly ladylike. She looks like a film diva to me and I like her very much. The other is a very expensive fortuneteller—I don't believe in it—who deals in art on the side. And the third, that's me. All three were once considered pretty in one way or another and were successful with men, and they all keep themselves in shape as best they can. They regret the unhurried loss of youth just a tiny bit, but one of them is extremely happy today, much happier than she used to be, and the same applies to me, the third one is struggling, and you can tell.

Late afternoon. The time has come. I have closed the book that is to be published. There is no turning back.
Now I can read the Sunday paper.

In the evening on TV, entirely unexpected, Edith Jud's wonderful film about the exciting and talented artist Dieter Roth. It was probably easier to shoot a film about the dead man than the living one. I remember him being pretty difficult, alcohol took its toll on him. A woman could never dare to be as embarrassing and uninhibited—whether on television or by setting up a camera in private, which has a touching aspect as well—no matter how talented she might be. And if she did it anyway, nobody would ever make a film about her later.
The artist's son plays a crucial role, rightfully so, because he's extremely charismatic, has a beautiful deep voice, but nonetheless possibly a tragic figure as the guardian of his father's oeuvre?
Because the film wouldn't have worked without him.

13 April

Chet Baker. I was still a schoolgirl when my first boyfriend—it was a very chaste relationship—drew my attention to this incomparable voice that has something feminine about it. Baker's songs have been lifelong companions. Once, young and naïve, I sent the musician a drawing in an Italian prison, long ago.

Then, shortly before he died, I actually ran into him in Zurich the day after a concert. He was alone and so was I. At long last I had the opportunity to confess to him how much he had meant to me for so many years.

I fall in love too easily,
I fall in love too fast.
I fall in love too terribly hard,
for love to ever last.

If someone were to ask me today about the greatest riches of my past, I catch myself thinking that maybe they were my encounters with men. Through them, I have learned so incredibly much. Through them, I have discovered so many different worlds, acquired so much insight into so many different ways of thinking: conventional, extravagant, sad as well, exuberant, desperate, cynical, and light footed.

By the way, there's not a single gate that leads more quickly and smoothly to the innermost chambers of fellow human beings than eroticism, I'm convinced of that. Often, after a single night of lovemaking, you basically know what a person is about. That's fascinating and I was addicted to it.

Being conquered didn't interest me; I wanted to do the conquering; I was the huntress and the collector.

Would that be different today?

Maybe these occasionally short and often longer affairs really were my greatest riches until later, much later, when I became capable of achieving happiness on my own.

It was, after all, the 1970s. A golden age of unbridled freedom. (Berlin and Paris had anticipated them in the 1920s.)

It was a time of rampant experimentation, of trying out different ways of life. Having fled the law in the United States, LSD pope Timothy Leary ended up in Zurich for a short time—hardly anyone was aware of it—and lived with a girlfriend of mine, one floor above me, in the same building I was living in. They were briefly a couple.

We were hoping, along with him, that certain drugs, in particular, of course, LSD, would change society, would foster a shift from materialism to spirituality.

The Salamander and I did not promise to be faithful to each other; we were faithful anyway and have been to this day, in a much deeper way.

At the time we indulged in or surrendered to all the experiments life had to offer, or maybe I should say, we sought them out and exposed ourselves to them. We were afraid of nothing and no one, we were totally identical in that respect. We were infinitely curious about people and experiences. We were constantly looking for something totally offbeat, for excess, and we collected people.

We had no secrets. The Salamander was my confidant, he knew exactly how and why I was driven.

Testing boundaries and above all transgressing them.

We ended up paying dearly for that.

Both of us.

And yet, at least in retrospect, I would do it over again.

It is unlikely that circumstances will ever permit people to live such hedonistic, unconstrained lives again. It was a brief window between the invention of the pill and the onslaught of AIDS.

Even politically, the hope of a future with less conflict prevailed.

It was a privilege to be young here in those days.

14 April

Women. They are important to me in an entirely different way from men. Some things I can tell only women. That's also why I would have liked to shoot "my" film with a woman. It's easier to work with women because there's no flirting involved; we see through each other and that's good. We don't have to play games, we know each other.

What a blessing that there are friendships between women. And that we can enjoy new friendships later in life as well. Women have given me so much and, above all, I learned about solidarity.

Currently, a woman my age and I are telling each other our lives, every day with a little more trust. That makes me realize how wonderful it is to have a past. Until recently, I rarely looked back.

For the first time this year, I have the impression that I have arrived.

Things are good the way they are.

Although I have to say that four women who played a role in my life at different times took their lives.

The middle-aged artist who took me by the hand and brought me to Zurich because she had fallen in love with me killed herself a few years later in her basement studio, by which time I was already married to my first husband. It was because of her last, unrequited love of a physician and mother of two or three small children; at the clinic, she already struck me as particularly appealing.
   "Life is an interesting experience, I do not regret it," the artist wrote.

Years later the artist was rediscovered, as it were, in connection with an exhibition at a Swiss museum, to which I also contributed a few pictures. Biographies have been written about her and she has since become well known. I spoke about her on television; I was then as old as she was when we met.

The young gallerist, whose very first exhibition showcased my *Salmon-Colored Boudoir*, immediately became the talk of the town because she was also very beautiful, and the girlfriend and muse of a well-known painter. I never quite understood why she started dressing like me—man's hat and trench coat, which was more or less my uniform—and trying to live as freely. She suffered from depressions, and one morning, it was a holiday weekend, she shot herself in the mouth with a gun. At a party the previous evening we had both curried the favor of the same man, I remember it so well, he was tall and blonde, and she got him. I never found out what happened that night.

The girlfriend, fashion stylist for a big store in Zurich: I had night-long conversations about love with her because we were both involved in a difficult relationship at the same time. She hanged herself above the bed of her lover. (Much later I did the fashion styling for a film by that man.) Oh, if only she could have stopped loving him. She no longer experienced how I finally succeeded in doing the same thing. Actually it was only after the breakup that I really started living!

Recently in conversation with a lovely acquaintance, the red-haired single who leads an exciting life and has become a sex consultant for a newspaper, we wondered about all the things she missed because she killed herself, all the exciting stories and nights of passion.

She herself has never been married and says she has a project, yes, that's exactly what she calls it, a project: she wants to get married no matter what.

But to whom?

The artist from Bern, striking and impossible to ignore, everybody told me I absolutely must meet her and everybody told her she must meet me, because we are so similar, and we kept trying and always missed each other. When we finally met up, we realized that our friends were right. We holed up for two or three weeks in my apartment in Zurich, didn't leave each other for a single second. Fifteen years later—by which time we met only rarely though she was still wearing the gypsy-ish clothing I had designed for her—she threw herself in front of a train.

That's the way it was.

All four women opted for the brutal, definitive, basically extremely male method, not like me, who was rescued. Although I always considered suicide a viable alternative as well.

Oh, I don't want to think of all the other people who already had to go.
   At least not today.

Tonight, in the park, the woman who feeds the swans told me that the same drama unfolds every year in the pond that is home to the extremely rare swans with the yellow beaks—and at the same time of year: one or two of the animals are attacked, caught, and end up in somebody's oven. This year the male swan managed to escape, his name is Moritz; now he is living out on the lake, and they didn't get the female either but broke so many bones with an iron rod that she couldn't be rescued and had to be put to sleep in the animal hospital.

If I were living in Rome or Berlin, I would do for cats what the woman did who collected bread for her swans. In Genoa, there were two simple women who cooked gigantic pots of spaghetti every day and brought them to homeless cats. I had daily responsibilities in that city, too, involving a lonely German shepherd, feral cats, and two neglected parrots in a pet store. Maybe I'll come back to that later. There were a few people-shy cats in Paris too, who sought out warmth in winter under the cars in a public parking garage and in the courtyard of the Cité des Arts, where I had a studio a couple of times; they would come at night to get their food.

Needless to say, I brought back one cat more than I had taken along when I left Switzerland to live in Italy for six months. She was very sick and had crawled under a parked car to die. On the other hand, it was another dog that I came back with from France. The Parisian.

The African dealers didn't show up in the park for quite a while with the exception of a man who looked lost and didn't seem well. They're back again today, four of them, not in their original spot but about 60 feet away near one of the big trees with low hanging branches that affords a good view of what's happening all around.

The Petite Fleur, the first official brothel in our city, the rooms of which I had planned to photograph, was supposed to be auctioned off today because the owner of the building from Wollishofen (not the manager I negotiated with) was so deep in debt. For reasons unknown the auction was canceled at the last minute.

15 April

The pond for the swans is actually empty. The sluice gate has been removed, they probably won't house birds there again.

The Petite Fleur has been sold, to a billionaire Swiss financier who is domiciled in South Africa. So business as usual.

Something must have happened to me this winter: I have solid ground under my feet. Never before have I felt like this, even though nothing particular has happened, nothing I could put my finger on.

Long, long ago I gave up believing that such a drastic change could be possible, ruled it out for myself. I thought a single lifetime was too short for that.

But fear is still breathing down my neck: what if it's only a passing phase?

16 April

As a teenager I read practically only French writers: François Mauriac to Henry de Montherlant, obviously André Gide and Jean-Paul Sartre, later Louise de Vilmorin and naturally Simone de Beauvoir, Georges Bataille, I was mad about Violette Leduc, the language of Marguerite Duras, it's actually music, it's still in my ears, I devoured Georges Simenon's mysteries, his biography is fascinating, and there's not a single book that I don't possess by Colette, in English and in German because she is the most sensuous writer I've ever read. It was my mother who told me about her when she died, I think, I was still a child.

The book I'm reading now, what a disappointment! Memories of the enigmatic and controversial writer Céline (*Voyage au bout de la nuit, Mort à crédit, Les Beaux Draps*). Recounted three or four years ago by his wife Lucette, well over eighty years of age, sick and dependent, a good forty years after the writer died. André Gide called him a genius. Lucette Almansor was a dancer, she is now close to death and one of the last to bear witness.

Louis-Ferdinand Céline was a doctor and a poet, a nihilist and a cynic, at least that's the image he cultivated, probably hated people, possibly an anti-Semite, although the latter is largely swept under the rug in France or at least disputed. In spite of all that, he often treated patients for free.

His books are largely autobiographical, maybe exaggerated. The then extremely famous actress Arletty (Marcel Carné's *Les*

Enfants du paradis with Jean-Louis Barrault) was a close friend of his. I even remember a picture taken when she visited him although he was no longer receiving guests, which made the photograph a minor sensation in France.

Once the American writer Charles Bukowski traveled especially to France and tried to visit him, Céline was his idol, but he was refused admittance.

There's another photograph I've cherished for years, picturing him in his slightly rundown house in Meudon, where he lived with Lucette and a lot of animals, dogs, cats, songbirds, and a parrot for the last 10 years of his difficult life. Oddly, a protagonist in one of his most famous books has the same name as a tomcat that he loved and took along on various journeys or escapes: Bébert. Who came first?

When I cut the photograph out, the idea of sharing my own life with animals was the farthest thing from my mind. But the appeal of the picture must have been related to that. It has long been part of my overflowing pinboard and so far I've never managed to put something else up in its place.

It pictures Céline a year before his death, smiling at his parrot who is clearly enjoying himself, nibbling on a fountain pen in his left claw, in the midst of the chaos on the writer's desk. There is an open birdcage behind him and an obviously unused fireplace of classical design around which notes have accumulated, some clothes-pinned to a grandfather clock. Lucette's smiling face can barely be distinguished in the mirror above the fireplace.

On the back there's a picture of the three-story Villa Maïtou, gloomy, with an equally neglected garden in front, Céline walking toward the photographer, his scarf billowing, Lucette in the background, wearing a dark floor-length dress, playing with a black standard poodle of almost eye-level height, the dog astonishingly fashionably coiffed.

It's so disappointing: you find out nothing in Lucette Almansor's book. Nothing about the human being Louis-Ferdinand Céline. So he will probably remain a mystery forever.

17 April
The filmmaker called to ask if I could gather more photographs that I have saved because they're important to me.

Because when still very young, I started saving newspaper articles. Clippings now yellowed that have been lying in boxes for years. Apparently they once moved me, and on re-reading them now, they still do.

Way down at the bottom of this collection, I come across a picture of a Parisian model named Marcelle Pichon, headlined "Ex-Model Kept Diary before Dying of Starvation." The slightly blurred picture shows a serious, bright, flat face with almond-shaped eyes and perfectly drawn eyebrows in the style of the 1950s, lipsticked mouth slightly open, teeth perfectly even. Her dark hair is combed back, probably in a chignon typical of fashion shows in those days, and with big clip-on earrings. The extremely yellowed clipping is from 1985 but the portrait of the person is 31 years old, apparently they couldn't find a more recent picture. The woman modeled for the famous couturier Jacques Fath in the 1950s. The caption tells me that she was exactly my age now when she starved herself to death, without anybody ever missing her. She had kept a kind of hunger diary that ended the day before her death on 7 November 1984. She was found in her apartment practically mummified—there's a picture of her—on 27 August 1985, so almost nine months later!
Such loneliness!

Or another equally yellowed and equally mysterious clipping, titled: "The Great Wardrobe of the Great Unknown Woman." It's about a vast collection of clothing that belonged to an unknown woman, consisting of some 1000, first-class haute couture items, including numbered models, which have already gone down in the history of fashion and originally cost up to Fr. 145,000. She must have been in the limelight a great deal because there were hundreds of evening dresses and at home she apparently wore negligées embellished with swan feathers. (I had one once, too; my beautiful artist husband is wearing it in a much-publicized picture of him dressed up as a kind of femme fatale.) Her wardrobe was supposedly stored in no less than sixty closets. No one knows who she was except that she had "a tragic accident in the prime of life," was German, and often lived in Montreux. The clothing dates from 1970 to 1984.

At the end of April 1984, there was supposedly a crime of passion near Montreux, in which a woman was killed by her lover who then killed himself. They both had wealthy partners, but were penniless themselves.

Quite a while ago I worked the following clipping into a small installation in my apartment:

"Russian dancer found dead. Wanted:
her mysterious young companion."

Unfortunately, the remainder of the text is missing. Pity. Stories like that inspire me.

Film material! Doing the research must be exciting. What a pity that my medium isn't film.

18 April

I'm meeting my girlfriend and her big dog with curly red hair, then the filmmaker, lunch at the lake.

Exhibition at the Kunsthaus of a very famous contemporary German painter, whose work fetches the highest prices in Europe, which means he has become a very rich man. We used to go bar hopping once in a while with him and other friends, all of us still penniless in those days. He was a heavy drinker and so were we. That has changed, and like some, but not all of us, he managed to find his footing before it was too late.

In that connection, I have a memory that's not very pleasant: shortly after one of my early performances, I had gone too far again and was lying sick, exhausted on a mattress on the floor in a girlfriend's apartment when a man lay down on top of me, held me tight, obviously wanting to take advantage of my weakness. Luckily somebody came in and threw him out of the apartment.

Later, years later, he became an interesting and even internationally famous artist.

The publisher's contract has to be completed and signed.

To submit the film for federal funding, photographs have to be selected and scanned.

I feel totally swamped today, papers that need to be filed piling up on my table, boxes full of old clippings that should be sorted and then put away again, but where? The biographer needs them and the filmmaker wants to see them, too.

I dream of somebody somewhere deciding to take care of the whole thing, maybe that will happen someday, who knows.

Same goes for endless files of negatives that I have never sorted through, let alone used...

19 April

"Buchalter's widow, wearing sunglasses and a veil, gives a press conference after her husband's execution."

This is the caption of another photograph I found in my papers. I can't date it anymore, but it's also on the pinboard in my workroom, to the right of the big red table.

It pictures a woman sitting at a round table covered with a white tablecloth. She has a beautifully shaped, slender face, light skin, dark red lips, pierced earrings. She is wearing sunglasses, the catlike shape curved up at the corners. Not too big to hide carefully plucked and penciled eyebrows.

Her dark hair, parted on the left, is combed back, to accentuate a cute little black hat, pillbox style, with a veil that almost reaches the glasses. She has a serious or maybe even slightly arrogant expression, and exudes confidence as she sits at the table, leaning casually on one arm with her hand dangling over the edge. In her other hand, with blood red fingernails and a costume jewelry ring, she is holding a sheet of paper, possibly the text of her communiqué. This figure, dressed in black, is in the middle of the picture, quite obviously the center of attention. Two men, their hair slicked back, are busily scribbling to her right. The body language of all five people in the photograph is crystal clear: because she is attractive and because she knows it, the wife of the executed man is in complete control of the situation and the men around her.

Another picture that I find enigmatic. Mystery writer Raymond Chandler would have liked it. How I would love to know more.

Saw a face at Bellevueplatz today, somehow familiar, an elderly woman with a cane, walking with great difficulty, a little overweight, round face, cortisone could be the cause. She was bent over, taking very short steps, she seemed sure nobody would recognize her. It was the first, now well over 70-year-old woman candidate for federal councilor—that was in 1983— and Social Democrat member of Congress until she retired four years ago. I wanted her to be elected to the Federal Council so badly and knew perfectly well she would never make it. The time wasn't ripe for it.

Is it any better now if you take a very close look? The way in which politically active women are sometimes treated today often suggests otherwise.

20 April
Our women's coffee klatsch this morning, always enjoyable and exciting.

Before that, a gardener explains every single tree along a stretch in the park, its age, its history, even its characteristics. He looked at every single tree with great devotion, indeed love, almost the way a man would look at a woman.

21 April
Ten different species of duck live in our lake. A sign tells me that there are pintails, teals, gadwalls, and mallards. As well as goldeneyes, tufted ducks, widgeons, spoonbills, common pochards, and red-crested pochards.

Then there are the birds that we call *Taucherli* (little divers): coots, little grebes, or dabchicks, great-crested grebes and goosanders.

And two kinds of seagulls, the bald gull and the common gull.

Larger birds include the heron and the cormorant.

There's also a unique individual, mustn't leave him out, a lone goose named Hans, I am told. I saw him for the first time last summer. Apparently, he belongs to someone at the other end of the lake and swims down to the city. He has made friends with a single swan, with Max, and together they come around noon to beg for a bit of bread from people lying on the meadow. Both little Hans and Max recognize their names and come swimming ashore when they are called.

Every year one of the most common ducks, a mallard, builds a nest in the bamboo of the sauna right next to our deck chairs. While we read our newspapers, she sits patiently and quietly on her seven to twelve eggs, for a full 28 days. Ordinarily, the young leave the nest soon after hatching. Sometimes one egg is left over.

The mother duck stays with her fledglings for some 50 to 60 days and they can fly after 7 to 8 weeks. Reading up on them, I learn that they can fly close to 70 mph and have a wing-span of some three feet wide.

Mallards are also native to North America, Asia, and Northwest Africa and inhabit all waters: lakes, rivers, and ponds. Their life expectancy is 10 to 15 years, but with human care, they can live as long as 40 years!

Like most birds, they are monogamous. Largely vegetarian, they feed mostly on leaves, grain, and seeds, but also like fruit, and, of course, the bread that we feed them. They will occasionally eat worms and insects.

More than once I have been stunned by something that is apparently not uncommon: a horde of drakes raping a female, grabbing her by the neck, and pushing her under water. The whole thing can take so long and cause so much injury that the female dies. Although the animals are monogamous, it seems there are often not enough females. I don't know why. Last year I had to watch how a female with five very small fledglings was systematically and repeatedly raped by six drakes, a heartbreaking spectacle that seemed endless. Her partner kept trying to chase the others away but with one against six, it was hopeless. Other people also had to watch, unable to do anything.

22 April
Telephone call from the filmmaker who asks about my earlier and current life. Challenging. I'm afraid that I have hardly any images to offer nowadays because my life is as unexciting as that of many others. It's about time!

But I like the filmmaker more and more. That's good.

He asked me which people are "important" to me or once had a place in my life.

Spontaneously, I think of a cultural philosopher, that's what he calls himself. He is still around, always in a good mood, everybody in Bern knows him. He recently curated an exhibition at the art museum there: Gerhard Johann Lischka. He witnessed my first forays into the art world and wrote about it in his publication, *Der Löwe* or *Die Löwin* (The Lion or The Lioness). You would see him at every important opening.

Same goes for the director Daniel Schmid. When I met him in the park recently, he told me how much he loved my work. We all know his films; unfortunately, he's not well.

Or the filmmaker I was friends with in those days, Reto Andrea Savoldelli. There's a lovely photograph of him in my kitchen, joined the anthroposophists in Dornach ages ago. He was already part of the "creative" scene in 1971 although not directly related to art, he left me drenched in tears after watching his wonderful film *Stella Da Falla* at the film festival in Solothurn.

Or the filmmaker Georg C. Radanovitch, who was a close friend of my artist husband and our wedding witness. It seems he's happily leading a private life in Aatal.

The multitalented artist Peter Schweri generously passed his ideas onto other artists and has since gone blind. Astonishingly, I never saw him depressed. I remember him working with a big magnifying glass and vastly enlarged pictures on the computer. Now he gives instructions to an artist colleague.

Or the notorious rock boss Tino, who promised he would always protect me because we were ultimately both outsiders: escaped from jail and dead. I'd rather not go into the reasons for his incarceration.

There was a whole clique that often hung out together, including the German artist Sigmar Polke, who often came to Zurich for longer times at a stretch, and the youngest rocker, at the beginning still almost a child, who called himself "Looser," as well as Peter Breslau, an attractive man who later became artist Susan Walder's partner. They all came to my art premiere. The photographer, art collector, and patron Andreas Züst was always there, too, and usually footed the bill. The day before his sudden, premature death in the year 2000, he supposedly bought a picture of mine from "my" gallery, apparently the last purchase he made.

The most striking male in those days, Baron Fredy von Beck, a young man of independent means, belonged to the same clique. He's the one who drove up in a Jeep when I had a breakdown after my first opening, picked me up at the Kontiki, and didn't let me out of sight day and night for a couple of weeks until I recovered. Has since died of an overdose, maybe killed himself, nobody knows.

The beautiful filmmaker Isa Hesse, married to Hermann Hesse's son, and mother of three grown children: in Paris I played a bit part, a woman in a wheelchair, in *Sirenen-Eiland*, which was later presented at the festival in Venice. There's a curious press photograph of me with Ines—Meret Oppenheim's lover at the time—taken in the catacombs. Just found the picture again on the Internet. Meret Oppenheim was living in a very small ground-floor apartment in Paris that she shared with Ines. Every morning Ines carried her mattress down to the cellar and up again every evening. (The love affair between the two did not end well.) We often sat together in charming, little, typically French bars, but without talking about art. Isa Hesse and Meret Oppenheim have since died. The German artist Ines-Irene Llosent y Gall, very proud of her beautiful name and one of Meret's first students, had a hard time getting over the separation.

Countless telephone calls—I had already long since returned to Switzerland—about it. Later she called herself "Hamburg's first violin." That appealed to me.

Or one of the most touching men in those days, hanged himself in a jail cell. I found out when I came back to Switzerland. He supposedly smuggled hash from Amsterdam to Switzerland. He had left me for an unknown girl. I was told that he suffered from claustrophobia.

He was still so young.

But back to the present.

A duck is actually brooding in the outdoor flower pot again, so close that you could reach out and touch her. Is it the same one every year?

Occasionally I come across one or two of the dark-skinned dealers in the park, sometimes here, sometimes there. They are obviously looking for a new strategy because they don't want to carry the stuff on them. Yesterday they checked out a bush outside of the park, located where it can be seen from two sides. At the former location near the rhododendron, there are two telltale mounds, somebody has apparently been digging. Business is largely done via cell phone, can't imagine how it used to be done.

23 April

The well camouflaged duck is sitting on nine eggs in her down-lined nest. I was able to count them when she came to eat softened bread straight out of my hand, she was obviously hungry. I'll continue feeding her, it's probably hard for her while she's brooding. I'll bring some greenery next time. In my studies about the life of ducks, I haven't found any mention of how they feed while they're brooding, and whether they leave the nest for that purpose.

But I do learn that couples already get together in the fall, courting until they mate in spring, and they can recognize each other from far away. The nest is upholstered with straw and twigs and down, the female builds it alone. The young all have the same brown camouflage color, whether male or female, probably a survival tactic since there are enemies. Here at the lake, it's probably mostly rats and crows as well as hawks. (At the beach there are currently several rat families; I see them in the semi-darkness raiding the garbage bags.) In late summer, the drake also molts—that

was new to me—it's called eclipse plumage
(what for?) and looks exactly like the female,
except for his yellow beak. Ordinarily his plumage is an iridescent green, especially his head,
with a white ring around the neck.

Waterfowl regularly lubricate their plumage
with their beaks; they take oil from the so-
called preen gland near their tails, and rub it
into their feathers with their beaks. I already
knew about that.

I also learn that "forced copulation" is not rare
and often fatal for the female.

24 April
The diary notes have been sent to the filmmaker, as always with great resistance and
reticence, even great embarrassment.

I have to cope with it.

Although we have long been in the new mil-
lennium, I noticed that many earlier memories
surface in the process of writing.

Tensely waiting to hear about the studio.

25 April
Meeting tomorrow morning with a friend who
was the very first to have the idea of doing a
Manon film, but did not succeed in getting

funding. Not because of the subject matter but because he comes from advertising and has no qualifications as regards making movies. He says he's totally depressed and has had no new plans since then.

The duck abandoned her eggs, she actually laid ten. Maybe I shouldn't have fed her? Did the spot seem too unsafe because of that?
I don't know.

In the evening, stopped in with my husband for an opening at "my" gallery. An artist is on view who became famous for inventing and designing a spectacular film figure plus context, for which he won the most important American film prize. But it didn't bring good luck because he has since been perceived more as a designer than an artist. Art museums still steer clear of him.
So he created his own museum, only for his own work. The public loves him, and his airbrushed work, mostly tone on tone, sells extremely well. A lot of people adore him almost like a saint, his posters embellish the rooms of countless teenagers.
There are a few quirky objects of a woman's genitals in his exhibition, very naturalistic, pretty and pink. I'd even consider buying one

of them if I were rich, although I don't like the artist's more popular pictures. They are dangerously close to kitsch.

Which is certainly not due to a lack of talent.

26 April
Just received a telephone call from a very elegant and no doubt vain girlfriend, she's just had cosmetic surgery. A test of courage. General anesthesia. A night at the hospital. I'm curious about the outcome. I can understand her. She's gone through life as a beauty and is not about to surrender hands down.

I hadn't noticed a single flaw in her appearance.

"She had reached an age at which one must pay more attention to overall appearance," Colette writes about one of her protagonists who was certainly leading an exciting life and had just turned 50.

Sooner or later, even the most beautiful women have to face transience. No one escapes.

What counts is whether there are other things to fall back on.

27 April
Back to the opening the day before yesterday: I remember that in connection with my first installation at Li Tobler's in 1974, there was an

exhibition with the motto: Manon, as seen by other artists.

The above-mentioned artist painted me together with my cat Minou, he called the picture *Minon* and it appeared on the cover of the journal *Metal Hurlant, hors-série, spécial Lovecraft*. It, too, was painted with a spray gun, predominantly in grays.

I've been told that people have had that exact same subject tattooed on their bodies. (I've even seen a photograph of it on a man's thigh.)

The tall, slender photographer from Bern, known for his oversized black-and-white pictures (he had already booked me to model for Helena Rubenstein cosmetics, to which an ad, an oversized photograph, testifies), wrapped me in snakeskin from the waist down, on my *Salmon-Colored* Bed. A very chaste photograph even though I'm bare breasted. He whimsically added a piece of genuine ocelot fur when he showed the picture.

He contributed to my very early black-and-white *Fetish Pictures* because, once when he came to visit, I was busy arranging and illuminating my objects and he wanted to try out a camera he had just acquired. That's how the cooperation came about. I have rarely exhibited the photographs, might be worth considering.

My second husband, usually alone in his photographed self-portraits, is pictured with me here, bending over me, probably to kiss me, I'm lying stretched out on a hammock, a very romantic motif. A vacation photograph, to be precise, taken in Italy at Lago d'Iseo, much enlarged in black-and-white on canvas. It was our last trip together. We felt it and loved each other very much and listened to Mina's songs nonstop and were very happy together, and at the same time indescribably sad.

Then there's a picture of my longtime artist friend from Zurich: it's an enlarged Polaroid in color. I'm sitting in a Jeep, the one belonging to Baron von Beck. He is bending over me, too, but in order to lift me out of the car. As I recall, I was wearing my white satin negligée decorated with Swan plumage.

The well-known artist from Bern added a drawing on paper. He not only draws and paints but also makes extremely tricky, poetic objects. Everyone will remember the object named *Eva*, consisting of three twigs. His picture of me was a small portrait painted after a photograph, before we had met. He later gave it to me.

It is through him that I met Wies Smalls, the famous art dealer from Amsterdam. In the show *Sentimental Journey* that I designed in 1979 for her gallery De Appel, I sat opposite each viewer, looking into their eyes for a certain amount of time. It felt as if half of Amsterdam had come, the crowd was so big there were long lines of people waiting and not everyone got a chance to enter. Even Marina Abramović, who later became famous, was there; she was also represented by the gallery.

It seems that the idea appealed to her.

I would have loved to have a picture of a then very young artist from Lucerne, who also used himself as the subject of his art, making travesties of himself in photographs and later to critical acclaim with an artist in Berlin. I remember the rooms of the commune very well in an old villa that subsequently became famous because of Franz Gertsch's pictures. I still have his colorful postcard self-portraits always addressed in red ink, glossy and with rounded corners.

The gallerist didn't want to exhibit him.
   A mistake.

Unfortunately I don't remember what the well-known and extremely provocative photo artist, who lives in Cologne, contributed. He also made himself the subject of most of his sexual and androgynous pictures, which caused a sensation and still do, rightfully so! An utterly idiosyncratic artist, I admire him a great deal. (He was also one of the "Transformers" a year later in Lucerne.)
   What a pity. Should inquire some time.

28 April
Got extremely lucky with an important fashion and advertising photographer. In addition to the mirrored cabinet with bed and canopy and thousands of objects, he photographed the performance *The Artist is Present* of twenty Manon doubles at the Rathaus in Lucerne, and also the installation *Philosophy in the Boudoir* with eight dissecting tables at my Zurich gallery and, it just occurs to me, also the show *Manon Presents Man* with seven real men seen in the windows of a former butcher's shop in Zurich-Höngg—all of that without ever charging me. Everything in color and giving me the slides afterwards. Thank you, dear Jost

Wildbolz! I will never forget that. The pictures have all been published several times and some were already reproduced in my very first little booklet.

Saturday. Library. Rain. Is there anything more pleasurable than lying in bed under a blanket with a pile of freshly borrowed books and listening to that sound? I could spend my life like that, another fifty years.

29 April

Every day is a good day, I once noted down. But today isn't. Partner problems are getting me down, always the same ones, we will never resolve them: he is a man and I am a woman, and so our view of the world is not the same.

Nonetheless, I sewed and readied my spring wardrobe, letting out or taking in seams. Sewing is one of the jobs I'm good at. In addition, I can do carpentry, plaster, paint, restore furniture, I like all kinds of manual crafts, I have nimble hands. I am also a good cleaning woman, quick and professional. I can cut hair, my own and that of my friends, who come especially to have that done.

I like my hands, because they are capable.

But I have no talent for cooking. Luckily, I've been able to organize most of my life so that I don't have to. In fact, I am generally bad at caring for people, I simply don't have the confidence.

I am incredibly shy.

But I'm a very good listener and quick to understand psychological situations. I probably wouldn't have been too bad as a psychiatrist. But I became an artist, apparently there was no getting around it.

30 April

Spent a few wonderful hours in the morning with a friend, the time flew.

Learned in the process, that if you put a sewing needle in a glass of water, it will invariably point north. It has to do with gravity, like a compass. My round window has morning sun, so it points east, and I see the sunset, the sun going down behind the Uetliberg, from my work table which points southwest.

An evening dip in the lake for the first time since my cold.

Then the summer: every single swimmer in our city knows that when the two church spires in Zurich overlap, they have reached the middle of the lake.

Once, only once in my life, two or three years ago, I went to Bern for the sole purpose of drifting in the Aare River. Unforgettable.

1 May

While rummaging through pictures for the film-maker in the cellar, came across gigantic, rolled up paintings, exactly as long as the long-est wall in the rooms of the studio in Genoa. Haven't unrolled them since, never looked at them again, never showed them to anybody, forgotten. They're very odd, good somehow, it would probably be worth exhibiting them. Someday someone will find them in all of my stuff, somebody will come up with the idea of showing them, who knows, maybe at some point every little scrap will be important.

And oh, these countless photographs down there in envelopes and drawers, it's getting out of hand, how am I ever going to sort them, get an overview?

For instance, a pretty voluminous series, never shown, of a model, namely, my current, photogenic husband at a very young age, sometimes with me, sometimes alone, some-times undressed, sometimes clothed, during another stay in a Parisian studio. So far I have only had one subject enlarged but have never shown it: we sit opposite one another on two chairs looking at each other, I am naked, he is wearing a suit and a tie. I have put my hand on his hand, and it is this gesture that brings the picture to life.

Pity.

Pretty soon our basement is going to look like artist Dieter Roth's studio with all his moldy items: namely, total chaos. I have to think of the story of the girl with her porridge that boiled over, rising over the edge, higher and higher and higher until it finally started bulging out of the house.

2 May

Meetings with one of my oldest friends are always based on mutual understanding and absolute honesty. We are both addicted to libraries and first met in one. We know each other very well and are similar. He met his partner, until recently a high-ranking cultural figure in Bern, in a museum in front of a picture of me, when they started a conversation and told each other that they were both acquainted with the artist. They've been together ever since.

Isn't that beautiful?

3 May
Walked barefoot outside today. May!

Now you can smell the fragrance again, these modest little white flowers growing on bushes, very sweet and at the same time vaguely musty. If I remember correctly, it lasts the whole summer until well into the fall.

4 May
While walking the dog, a man comes towards me on a unicycle, right at the water where you have to concentrate especially hard to keep your balance on the big stone blocks. But we still smile at each other. I see myself in him: that's exactly how I used to go through life, acutely aware of a potential fall.

One morning last summer I saw a drake staggering across the street; it's a miracle he didn't get run over. I caught him and emptied out our bathroom. I discovered a wound on his neck, probably a dog bite. He surrendered completely to having the wound dressed. It was almost devastating to see how he submitted to his fate in this windowless room. A few days later he had recovered enough to be returned to the lake. I put him in a closed basket to carry him to the lake and the closer we came the more excited he got. It was beautiful to see how happy he was to plunge into his element again and most likely return to his lady duck. For a while after that, every time I saw a drake I wondered if it was "mine."

The bathroom was full of droppings and full of beautiful feathers.

5 May
Met the filmmaker.

Still the same question: just exactly what is he supposed to film? My days are so marvelously unspectacular.

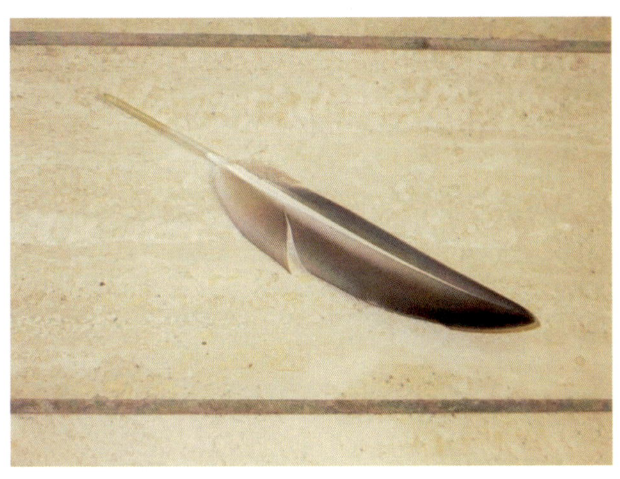

6 March 2019
My first husband died at seven-thirty this morning. He was a friend until the end.
The lake is beautiful as usual.
A cormorant is spreading its wings in the wind.

MANON

Artist.
Photographs, performances, installations,
exhibitions at home and abroad.
Prix Meret Oppenheim (2008), among others.
Lives in Zurich.

MANON, *FEATHERS*

Text: Manon
Translation: Catherine Schelbert
Copy editor: Elizabeth MacFadyen
Proofreading: Louise Stein

Book design: Marietta Eugster
Assistance: Célestine Claudin
Prepress: Aron Fluri
Printing and binding: Musumeci S.p.A.
Paper: Lessebo Design
                             Smooth Natural 90 g
Cover: Invercote Albato 270 g
Font: Riforma LL, NORM

First edition: Edition Patrick Frey,
                             2020

Print run: 800 copies
ISBN: 978-3-907236-10-9
                             Printed in Italy

© 2020 photograph: Manon
© 2020 text: Manon
© 2020 for this
   edition: Edition Patrick Frey

Edition Patrick Frey
Limmatstrasse 268, CH – 8005 Zürich
editionpatrickfrey.com
mail@editionpatrickfrey.ch

DISTRIBUTION

Switzerland	AVA Verlagsauslieferung CH – Affoltern am Albis ava.ch
Germany, Austria	GVA Gemeinsame Verlagsauslieferung D – Göttingen gva-verlage.de
France, Luxembourg, Belgium	Les presses du réel F – Dijon lespressesdureel.com
United Kingdom	Antenne Books GB – London antennebooks.com
United States	Artbook / D.A.P. USA – New York artbook.com

Japan	Twelvebooks JP – Tokyo twelve-books.com
Australia, New Zealand	Perimeter Distribution AU – Melbourne perimeterdistribution. com
Rest of the world	Edition Patrick Frey CH – Zürich editionpatrickfrey.com

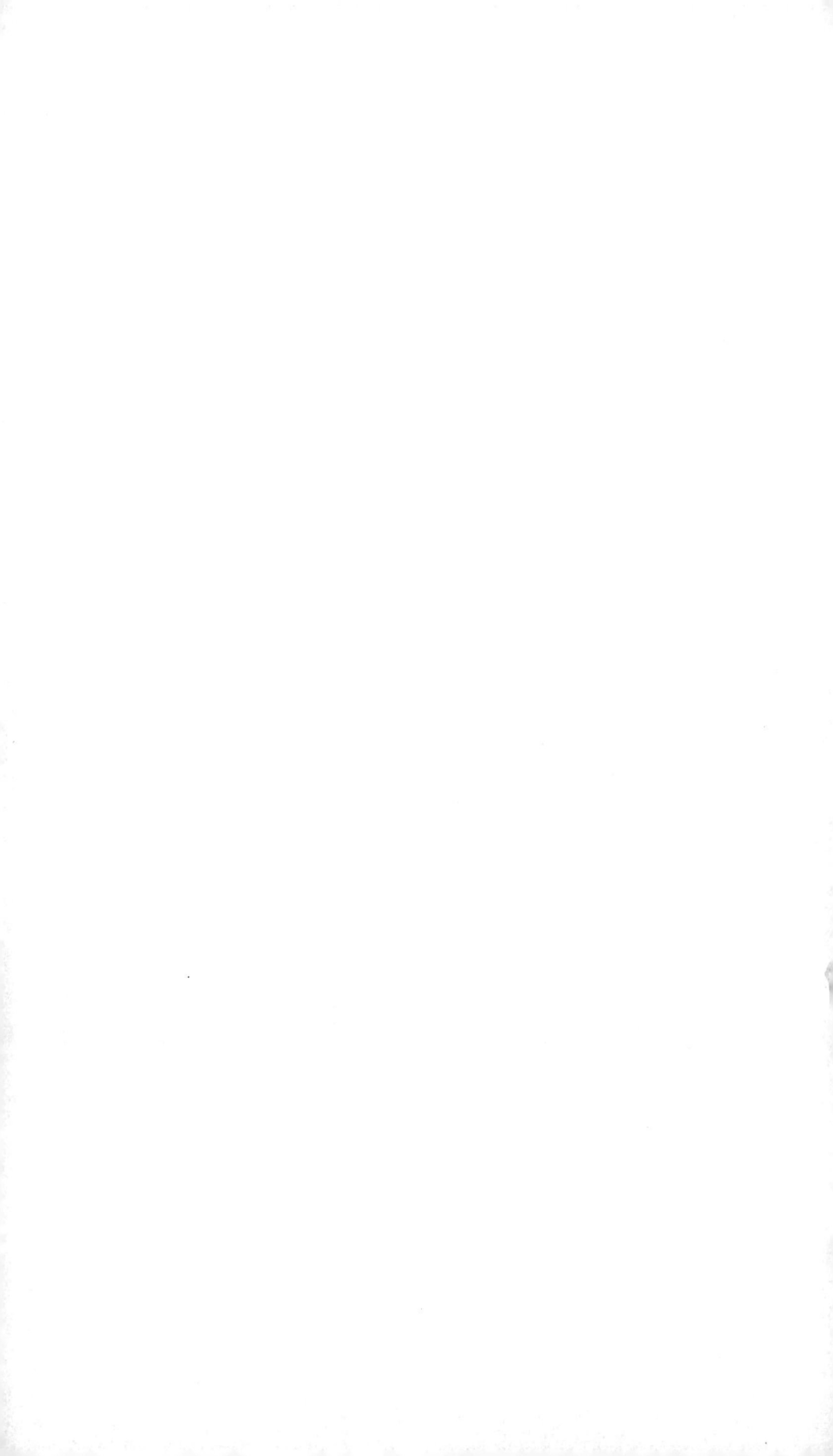